HUGUENOT
GALLEY
SLAVES

Jean Martielhe

"Looking unto Jesus
the author and finisher of our faith;
who for the joy that was set before him
endured the cross, despising the shame,
and is set down at the right hand of
the throne of God."

Hebrews 12:2

THE HUGUENOT GALLEY SLAVES

Taken from the Memoirs of
Jean Martielhe

As included in a history of
the French Protestants by
Johann Jacob Rambach
1693-1735
Published Originally in French

1759

Edited and abridged by
Rev. Christian G. Barth, D.D.
1799-1862

2011 Edition
From the Presbyterian Board of Publication Edition
Edited, updated, and footnotes & illustrations added by

Hail & Fire
www.hailandfire.com

"The Huguenot Galley Slaves," taken from the Memoirs of Jean Martielhe, as included in the 1759 history of the French Protestants by Johann Jacob Rambach, edited and abridged by Rev. Christian G. Barth, D.D. and published in English by the Presbyterian Board of Publication in a 19th century edition, is herein reprinted with edits, updates, footnotes, and illustrations added by Hail & Fire.

ISBN-10 0982804342
ISBN-13 978-0-9828043-4-6

Hail & Fire is a resource for Reformed and Gospel Theology in the works, exhortations, prayers, and apologetics of those who have maintained the Gospel and expounded upon the Scripture as the Eternal Word of God and the sole authority in Christian doctrine. "By manifestation of the truth commending ourselves to every man's conscience in the sight of God." 2 Corinthians 4:2

www.hailandfire.com

For posterity, but
most especially for the
children of God.

CONTENTS

PREFACE
to an ancient edition

 ear Reader, here is a little book for your perusal. It is not adapted for mere amusement, and I think you will find it both interesting and instructive. Our path of life is not always equally smooth. We must expect to encounter difficulties and sometimes even dangers. Should you ever be exposed to persecutions similar to those of these youths, this little book may afford you much warning and encouragement; and if you are preserved from such trials, it may show you how grateful you ought to be for your great and precious privilege!

The following narrative is extracted from Rambach's history of the French Protestants published in the year 1760, having been first published in French in the year 1759.

I have added nothing of my own to the contents of this work, but have given the account just as I found it, except that I have been obliged to omit much that is interesting, otherwise I would have made it too long for you. As it is, I hope that it will afford you both pleasure and improvement.

Rev. Christian G. Barth

PREFACE
to the modern edition

ike previous editors and publishers, we have chosen this little book for reprinting as it is material true to history, and it is thus intended for serious consideration. While the story itself, like any grand adventure, is very engaging, the facts of this history in the relationship between men and creeds, especially related to the original faith of Jesus Christ, are of paramount consequence. It may be said that history is the proof and the evidence itself left to us by which we may judge of the truth, of the godliness, and of the holiness of those systems of belief held by those who went before us. It is Jesus Christ who teaches all men to test all things according to a simple rule: "You shall know them by their fruits. Do men gather grapes of thorns, or figs of thistles? Even so every good tree brings forth good fruit; but a corrupt tree brings forth evil fruit," Matthew 7:16-17.

If we then test those faiths and creeds by their fruits, by the evidences of history, by events and consequences, by how the rights of religion and speech and conscience are respected and conceded or abrogated and abolished, and study to learn how power is wielded over the lives of men, we shall have gleaned for ourselves the greatest truth of right and wrong, and of darkness and light as it is found in the creeds of men. We see on the one hand, oppression and power, and on the other hand, strength, faith, godliness, care for the essential truths of the Gospel, and a constant gracious faith that is stayed upon Jesus Christ.

Let us not look to the past to whitewash it, for the past is a record of the very trial of men's creeds and it is the record itself afforded to all that we might examine and judge the fruits of the religions and doctrines that men live by in this world. All men, men of every creed, in the words of that famous Protestant historian and martyrologist, Alexis Muston, "must endure history to the last."[1]

Hail & Fire
Jan. 2011

---

1. Alexis Muston, *The Israel of the Alps; History of the Vaudois of Piedmont*, 1857 Edition.

NOTE
regarding the modern edition

n the preparation of this little book, we attempted to locate an original edition of Rambach's history of the French Protestants, in order to replace those names of persons, cities, and places that were omitted in subsequent editions, that is, if the record of them was indeed ever published by our author, but our search for a copy of the volume was without success.

The original, however, a volume of Memoirs by Jean Martielhe, from which Rambach took his history, we did locate. Jean Martielhe is the true name of our author, who identifies himself only as John Mantel in the narrative. This substitution of names occurred at the time the story was originally published and was likely made by the original author in order to protect, in so volatile a time, those mentioned in the history.

In our edition, compared to that from which we took our text—the abridged edition by Rev. Christian Barth—we have replaced the abbreviated and missing names and reinserted the true. This includes the city of origin of the narrator, John Mantel, or rather, Jean Martielhe, and his companion, Daniel le Gras, for which we have replaced that given as "B" with Bergerac, which is in the province of Perigord; the name of the

Duke of "F," which we have replaced with the Duke de la Force, which Duke took up to compel the Huguenots to become Catholics in the areas of southern France, where our story begins; and the place of "P" with Perigord from which the Duke commenced these proceedings; one of the villages, "M" we have replaced with the original Mussidan, which our fugitives passed through after leaving Bergerac en route to what was their original destination of Holland; and Mr. Piecourt for M. "P," the rich banker at Dunkirk. It should be noted that all other names were provided by our author and are original to the text of the Memoirs including the river Mêuse, Mezières, Charleroi, Couvé, the friendly M. de la Salle, the irritated M. de la Brillière, the Royal Galleys at Dunkirk, the names of the ships Commanders, Havre, Marseilles, and the rest.

To trace the path of Jean Martielhe and his companion, Daniel le Gras, from their start in southern France, in the year 1700, en route to Holland and ultimate freedom, through their arrest and imprisonment, and then to enslavement in the Royal French Galleys at Dunkirk and at Marseilles, turn to the Map which appears in this edition. We have also indicated on our Map the route by which our author traversed France en route to Holland a second time, after more than ten years of slavery for the sake of the Gospel, when at last, in 1713, freedom was won for the Protestant Galley slaves through the aid and intercession of the Protestants of Europe; for, our author does not just arrive at the Hague in Holland, but gains that land after so much assistance and common rejoicing together with the various Protestant churches from Nice, to Turin, to Geneva, Berne, Frankfort, and then to Rotterdam and Amsterdam where he is asked to join the party of freed Huguenot slaves who were sent to London to the very

Queen who was so instrumental in bringing about their release and liberty.

We have also included a brief *Historical Background* to the events of this story. To read more about the history and the personal and true stories of those who endured the scourge of inquisitions and crusades, including the Huguenots, the Lollards, the Calvinists, the Waldenses, the Vaudois, and so many other Protestant peoples who suffered ecclesiastical and civil penalties against that pure and Gospel faith, we have included at the back of this book a list for *Further Reading*.

HISTORICAL BACKGROUND

t was Henry IV, King of France, who, in 1598 published the Edict of Nantes, granting toleration to the long persecuted Protestants of France, commonly known as Huguenots. The Huguenots differed only from the Waldenses and Vaudois, in that the Huguenots were persons formerly of the Catholic faith, having left that Church in the great departure of the Protestant Reformation; the Waldenses and Vaudois had never been a part of it.

The French Protestants, says the Roman Catholic historian Jaques-Auguste De Thou, councilor to King Henry III and Henry IV of France during the era just prior to our story, were given "the ridiculous and odious name of Huguenot," *"le nom ridicule & odieux de Huguenot."*[1] The heretics of France had, for some time been called "Huëts les Herétiques" of the country,[2] being the same, he says, as those who were before called Lutherans. These new Lutherans, *"nouveaux Luthériens,"* continues De Thou, were growing in numbers day by day,[3] in spite of the threatenings and efforts against them.

---

1. De Thou, *Histoire Universelle*, 1742 Edition, Vol. III, p. 766.

2. *"On a long-tems appellé en France Huëts les Herétiques du pais."* ibid.

3. *"Les Protestans, dont le nombre devenoit plus grand de jour en jour."* ibid., p. 705.

The Waldenses and Vaudois, who were the Gospel believing peoples that inhabited the most remote valleys and mountains of Europe, had held and maintained the original and apostolic doctrine and scriptures entirely outside the influence or control of the Roman Catholic Church—the papacy and the Catholic tradition, from the earliest centuries of the Christian era and throughout the entirety of the Middle Ages. After the Reformation, the peoples of the pre- and post-Reformation Protestant creeds blend in perfect fellowship, remaining distinguishable only by their more ancient or modern affiliations, locations, and the derisive names assigned to them by those who persecuted them.

The name Huguenot, says another source, appears to have been a popular corruption of the German 'eidgenossen' or 'conspirators.' The close connection of the French Protestants to those in Geneva and elsewhere, who were called 'Eidgenossen,' led to their first being called by this term in the Touraine in about 1550 under the form of 'Eigenots,' which became 'Huguenots.' "This name," so it is said, "the people applied in hatred and derision to those who were elsewhere called Lutherans, and from the Touraine it spread through France."[1]

The Huguenots, together with the Waldenses, the Vaudois, the Lollards, and the various Protestant peoples across Europe, were continually subject to the most severe ecclesiastical and civil penalties, crusades, massacres, and inquisition. At the time of our story, the French court wavered between using these methods against the French Protestants and, when the numbers of them increased and their strength was great, efforts

---

1. *The Catholic Encyclopedia*, 1910 Edition, Vol. VII.

to make peace in order to safeguard their position and power.

In 1559, when Pius V came to the Pontifical office,[1] he, with "an intense, unmitigated detestation of Protestantism, and a fixed, inexorable determination to root it out," occupied himself continually sending money and soldiers to France, and letters to the kings and bishops across Europe inciting them to zeal in the ruin of the heretics. To the commander of his military force, Count Santafiore, according to Catena, he had given the instruction "to take no Huguenot prisoner, but instantly to kill every one that fell into his hands."[2]

Pope Pius V.

In 1569, however, despairing of the destruction of the Huguenots in France, Pius suggested a more secret and sure way for their eradication. In a letter to the Cardinal of Lorraine, the Pope wrote, "use all your influence for procuring

---

1. Michael Ghislieri, previous to becoming Pope Pius V, was a Dominican and an Inquisitor in the Piedmont and in Rome.

2. "Pio se dolse del Conte che non havesse il comandamento di lui osservato d' ammazzar subito qualunque heretico gli fosse venuto alle mani." Leopold Ranke, *The Popes of Rome: Ecclesiastical and Political History of the 16th & 17th Centuries,* Vol. I, p. 258, from *Vita di Pio V.*

a definite and serious adoption of the measure most proper for bringing about the destruction of the implacable enemies of God and the King." And to the King, Charles IX, who was the son of King Henry II and Catherine de Médici, he wrote an exhortation to "pursue and destroy all the enemies that still remain." "For unless they are radically extirpated, they will be found to shoot up again." "You will not succeed," he tells Charles, "in turning away the wrath of God, except by avenging him rigorously on the wretches." The Pope then presented himself as the prophet Samuel delivering the message to Saul—Charles IX, to destroy the Amalekites—the Huguenots, utterly.[1] To Catherine, the Pope wrote plainly, advising that she pursue the "enemies" until "they are all massacred, for it is only by

Charles IX, King of France.

---

1. A reference to 1 Samuel 15, the implication being that the king may not refuse to obey the Pope or spare any Protestant for any cause, as Saul's error was his having taken "Agag the king of the Amalekites alive, and utterly destroyed all the people," for which cause God also rejected Saul and took the kingdom of Israel from him (1 Samuel 15:23-28). This was no idle threat: after the death of Charles, his younger brother Henry succeeded to the throne and was himself excommunicated by the Pope and accordingly assassinated as commanded in the bull of excommunication.

the entire extermination of heretics *(deletis omnibus)* that the Roman Catholic worship can be restored."[1]

From that moment, the design of what became known as the St. Bartholomew's Day Massacre began. Several years in the planning, the intended massacre was set to begin in Paris and resound, according to the will of the King and the zeal of the Catholic populace, throughout the provinces of France. Necessarily then, the Protestant rulers must be lured under pretext to the city and soldiers and people prepared to strike. The wary Protestants, however, having signed so many pacts of peace with the French court, were not easily lured. Catherine de Médici, who had demanded before the Pope that the timing and execution of the plan be left to herself, contrived to marry her daughter, Margaret de Valois, to the young King Henry III of Navarre. This plan,

Catherine de Médici.

carried out for all its worth, was designed to raise the hope of a real and substantial peace for the Protestants, and to ensure that the last of them fell in the slaughter.

In August of 1572, four days after the wedding was held at the Cathedral of Notre Dame in Paris, the bells began to toll in order to arouse the citizens, who had been previously armed for the occasion. To ensure

---

1. Rev. J. A. Wylie, *History of Protestantism*, from *Epp. Pii a Goubau*, the secretary to the Spanish Embassy at Rome, published in 1640.

that the citizenry acted with violence at the moment the signal was given, a plot had been fabricated and word spread among the people, that the lives of the royal family had been threatened by the Protestants. Obediently, then, upon hearing the first warning bell, shots began to ring out and the people set themselves to the massacre of all who were of the Protestant faith. The butchery continued for two months throughout the provinces of France and, according to Perefixe, the Archbishop of Paris, the death toll reached 100,000 persons.

The St. Bartholomew's Day Massacre,
which began in Paris in 1572.

Charles IX lived less than two years after this horrible scene, having reigned from 1560-1574 and dying at the age of only twenty-four. Reportedly he experienced a fearful remorse at the recollection of the deeds of the

St. Bartholomew's Day Massacre. On his deathbed, Charles, being waited upon by his nurse, fell into tears and through his sobs said, "Ah nurse, dear nurse, what blood, what murders! Ah, I have followed bad advice. Oh, my God, forgive me! Have pity on me, if it please thee. I do not know what will become of me. What shall I do? I am lost; I see it plainly." The nurse, a Huguenot, said to the king, "Sire, may the murders be on those who made you do them; and since you do not consent to them and are sorry for them, believe that God will not impute them to you, but will cover them with the robe of his son's righteousness. To him alone you must address yourself."[1]

On the death of Charles, his younger brother, Henry, Duke of Anjou, ascended the throne as King Henry III. Henry III reigned 15 years, from 1574-1589, at the end of which he was excommunicated by the Pope who urged his immediate assassination; this deed, a monk named Jacques Clement, dutifully performed. Catherine herself expired the same year. The youngest heir, Francis, Duke of Alençon, having adopted the cause but not the religion of the Protestants, had died of a fever five years before.

Against all odds, it is King Henry III of Navarre, a Protestant, who then succeeded to the throne of France, bringing the Valois line to an end and establishing the Bourbon line of rulers over that country. Henry IV reigned from 1589-1610, and although a Protestant, he came to the throne of a France yet entangled in religious persecutions, factions, and murders; a France where Protestant children were taken from their parents and educated as Catholics; where the legal wills of Protestant citizens were made void, and where great

---

1. Rev. J. A. Wylie, *History of Protestantism*.

outrages were still being committed upon that people. Rather than taking up the noble task of ending the persecutions by establishing freedom, justice, and equity for all men, Henry IV looked to gain the admiration of the Catholics and took upon himself to play a double part, receiving instruction in the Catholic catechism, while holding the Protestants at arm's length. To their every entreaty, Henry insisted that freedom must wait until such a moment as he was more firmly established upon the throne.

Henry IV, King of France, who, in 1598, issued the Edict of Nantes, granting freedom of conscience to all.

"And yet, sire," they replied, "among us we have neither Jacobins[1] nor Jesuits who aim at your life, nor Leagues who aim at your crown. We have never presented the points of our swords instead of petitions. We are paid with considerations of State policy. It is not time yet, we are told, to grant us an edict—yet, Oh merciful God, after persecution and banishment! We ask your Majesty for an edict by which we may enjoy that which is common to all your subjects. The glory of God alone, liberty of conscience, repose to the State,

---

1. A society of revolutionaries in France, who took their name from their monastery.

security for our lives and property—this is the summit of our wishes, and the end of our requests."

From 1589 until 1598 they continued to wait, until at last, Henry, about to lose his crown to the very League cited, was in need of the Protestants to support and protect that crown. On April 15, 1598, that famous decree known as the Edict of Nantes[1] was issued, granting "Full liberty of conscience to all," with express permission granting those of the Reformed faith the free exercise of their religion, the right to hold public office, to be admitted to schools and hospitals and their poor to be cared for by public alms, and allowing them to print Protestant and Reformed literature "in certain cities." For the future protection of Protestant interests, courts were to be erected which were composed of an equal number of Protestants and Catholics.[2]

It may be pointed out that it was not the persecution and suppression of the Protestant religion, nor the apostasy or duplicity of Henry, but the Edict of Nantes and the granting of religious liberty to all men that brought about peace, safety, and prosperity within the realm of France. Seeing the immediate effects of the Edict, Henry took up in earnest the office of statesman in the cause of France, and over his remaining years, reduced the public debt and government spending and encouraged commerce, agriculture, industry, and free trade, achieving not only peace but prosperity within the realm. The life of Henry IV was cut short in 1610 by a monk named Francois Ravaillac, who stabbed the King as he rode in his carriage, because, said he, "he was too favorable to heretics."

---

1. Nantes is the city in western France from which the Edict was published.

2. Rev. J. A. Wylie, *History of Protestantism.*

Henry's son, a boy of eight, ascended the throne as Louis XIII, and the former edicts of toleration were quickly ratified and the Huguenots assured that no change in policy was to be feared. However, under the regency of his mother, Maria de Médici, and through the intense Catholic influence of the Pope and clergy, the young king was distanced from his father's policy and allied to those who would silence anyone who might question the Church and the Pope. By 1614 the Supreme Parliament of France openly affirmed that the king was under oath to exterminate heretics; clergy and nobles discounting all pleas for toleration. The previous edicts and treaties with the Huguenots, they said, were provided only because king and court could do nothing else at the time. By 1617, a Dragoonade,[1] was sent to reduce Navarre, which was largely Protestant, to submission to the Catholic religion. The Pope, having absolved the king of all conscience regarding past promises to the Huguenots, provided millions of crowns to finance the new efforts against Protestantism in France. It was under Louis XIII that Cardinal Richelieu became master of France and placed the Huguenots under an 'edict of grace,' virtually overthrowing the Edict of Nantes only twenty years after the Edict was originally signed.

Upon the death of his father in 1643, Louis XIV, came to the throne of France as a child of four. In his majority, Louis was an ambitious and powerful king. As early as 1661, he sought every method to limit the application of those concessions which his grandfather, Henry IV, had granted to the Protestants by the Edict of Nantes.

---

1. To 'dragoon' is the tactic of abandoning a place to the violence of a dragoonade, a troop of dragoons or musketeers on horseback, in order, by such violence, to reduce the populace to submission.

A Dragoonade.

In about 1680, Louis XIV began a more aggressive policy toward the Huguenots. His licentious lifestyle had rendered Louis particularly subject to the guilt and

penances heaped upon him by the Catholic priests. At their instigation, his chief goal became the extirpation of Protestantism in France, in order to both satisfy his oath as king and to fulfill the penances imposed upon him by his confessor.[1] As the historian Rev. J. A. Wylie, has said, designing to atone his sins "by the sacrifice of the Huguenot heretics."

King Louis XIV of France, who issued the Revocation of the Edict of Nantes in 1685.

Thus began the process of divesting the Protestants of the rights that they had been granted under the Edict of Nantes. From this time, every complaint was settled in favor of the Catholic party; Protestants lost their churches, schools, and charitable institutions to the Catholic Church; relapsed heretics were banished for life; and ordinances were passed to ensure that priests alone were allowed to visit the sick and dying. Protestant parents were compelled to place their children in Roman Catholic schools and homes at the age of seven and to pay for

---

1. The priest who heard the king's confessions and had the power to grant absolution and remission of his sins.

their maintenance. Any preacher, who spoke against the Catholic saints or the Virgin Mary, was indicted for blasphemy. Protestant preachers were given a fortnight to leave the country on pain of the Galleys; and Protestants were again excluded from public offices and from the practice of law and medicine.

In spite of these measures, the priests cried for more zealous efforts "to cause the formidable monster of heresy to expire completely." Dragoonades were accordingly sent out, beginning with Poitou, and as many as four to ten soldiers were quartered on each Protestant family with full license to do as they pleased in order to force a conversion to the Catholic religion.

Persecution of the Huguenots.

In all places in France terror reigned and the people were entirely in the hands of ruffians. "Not a post arrives," wrote Madame de Maintenon,[1] in September, 1685, "without bringing tidings that fill him (the king) with joy; the conversions take place every day by thousands."[2]

---

1. Madame de Maintenon was the King's mistress and was secretly married to the king some time after his wife died.

2. Rev. J. A. Wylie, *History of Protestantism.*

At the advice of his confessor, on October 18, 1685, Louis XIV signed the Revocation of the Edict of Nantes. Protestants fled the country *en masse* and those who made it across the border were welcomed into

Revocation of the Edict of Nantes in
1685 under Louis XIV.

nearby countries on account of their piety and industry. The use of Dragoonades was extended to the southern provinces of France. Those Huguenots who fled in the Cevennes and the Pyrenees were tracked and made to convert or suffer death. "Neither the decrepitude of old age nor the pleading weakness of infancy stirred any remorse in the breasts of the bloody butchers who went about cutting down all ages, sexes, and conditions."[1] All Protestant churches and books were destroyed, and all

---

1. John Clark Ridpath, *History of the World*, 1914 Edition, Vol. VI, p. 452.

Bibles were burned. The Protestants that were made to convert were given the name "New Catholic" and were instructed in the Catholic religion.

In an attempt to stop the exodus of Protestants that fled from France—from the revived policy against them and from the Dragoons that were sent among them—the king threatened all fugitives with slavery for life on the Royal French Galleys.[1]

> And here is where the story of John
> Mantel, or *Jean Martielhe,* begins.

---

1. Rev. J. A. Wylie, *History of Protestantism.*

MAP

Of the travels of John Mantel, or Jean
Martielhe, & his companion, Daniel le Gras.

ur map follows the travels of our chief narrator, John Mantel or rather, Jean Martielhe, and his companion, Daniel le Gras, who, in 1700, fled the persecution of the Protestant Huguenots in France, which began as a result of the Revocation of the Edict of Nantes by King Louis XIV. Their journey quickly takes them to prison and, from 1702-1713, to slavery on the Royal French Galleys. In 1713, freedom was won for the Protestant Galley slaves through the intercession of the Protestant Princes of Europe. Our story progresses as follows:

- Bergerac, a city in southern France.

- 1700. Journey to Paris en route to freedom in Holland.

- Over the river Mêuse & into Mezières; to Charleville, Rocroy & then through a mountain pass & into Couvé, near the Forest of Ardennes & beyond the French frontier.

- Detour to Marienburg.

- 1701. Arrest at Marienburg.

- Journey to the prison in Tournay - passage on foot through Philippeville, Maubeuge, and Valencienne.

- ▷ Imprisonment at Lisle.

- ▷ Transfer to the state prison in Tournay.

- ▷ Transfer back to the prison at Lisle.

- ▷ Journey by cart to Dunkirk to the Royal French Galleys.

- ▷ 1702. Enslavement on the Royal French Galleys, sailing against English and Dutch ships; near shipwreck in the bay at Ambleteuse, between Calais and Boulogne.

- ▷ 1712. To the hospital in Dunkirk; and transfer from rowing to clerk because of injuries received in battle.

- ▷ Transfer to Marseilles via Havre de Grace, Charenton, Isle of France, Burgundy, and Mâçon, to Lyons, by boat up the Rhone to den Heiligen Geist, & by land to Avignon & then Marseilles.

- ▷ Enslavement on the Royal French Galleys at Marseilles.

- ▷ 1713. Freed by command of King Loius XIV, who, at the insistence of the Protestant Princes of Europe freed the Huguenot Galley slaves.

- ▷ By boat to Nice & by mule through the mountains to Turin, and then on to Geneva.

- ▷ From Geneva to Berne & on to Frankfort.

- ▷ 1713 (August). Frankfort & Bochenheim.

- ▷ Upriver from Frankfort to Cologne, by boat to Dort and then to Rotterdam & Amsterdam.

- ▷ To London to thank & petition Queen Anne.

- ▷ From London to the Hague.

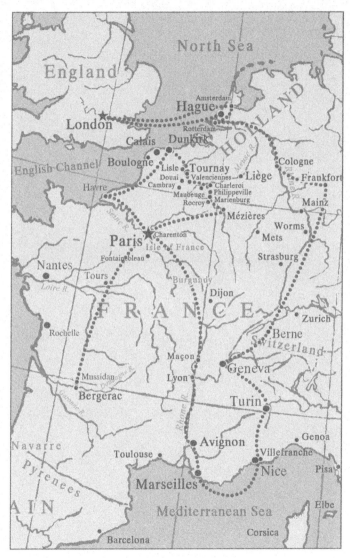

MAP
The travels of John Mantel (Jean Martielhe).

CHAPTER 1
INTRODUCTION

CHAPTER 1
INTRODUCTION

enry IV, King of France, had by the publication of the Edict of Nantes in the year 1598, secured for his Protestant subjects not only the free exercise of their religious worship, but had also granted to them, in common with the Roman Catholics, the power of holding offices and dignities of state. But his grandson, King Louis XIV, having resolutely determined to subvert[1] Protestantism in France, began, as early as the year 1660, to violate the privileges of the Huguenots,[2] and from that time he continued to make greater inroads[3] upon their religious liberty until, in 1685, he revoked the Edict of Nantes which had secured it.

In consequence, the Reformed clergy were immediately banished, and those provinces through which the mountains of the Cevennes extend—the departments of Gard, Lozère, and Ardêche[4]—and where the greatest number of those who professed the Reformed faith

---

1. To overthrow.

2. The name given to the Protestants in France *(see the "Historical Background" for more information on the origin of this name).*

3. Encroachments.

4. These departments still exist and are in the southernmost central area of France: Gard is in the province of Languedoc-Roussillon, Lozère is in Massif Central, and Ardêche is in the Rhone Valley-French Alps.

lived, became the scene of the most savage barbarity and horrible outrages.[1] Dragoons and other soldiers were sent into these provinces in order to compel the unfortunate inhabitants to renounce their faith. The persecution was so oppressive that numbers of Huguenots were induced to yield a quick submission in order to escape the violence. About five hundred thousand persons, abandoning the greatest part of their

Medal struck by Louis XIV in 1685 in honor of the Revocation of the Edict of Nantes. The inscription reads, "Templis Calvinianorum Eversis," "The Churches of Calvin Overthrown in Ruins."

personal property, fled these regions and sought refuge in the neighboring Protestant countries. Those who remained, after patiently having endured seventeen years of the most inhuman treatment, at length determined to resist their enemies and took up arms in their own defense.

---

1. "The policy was to 'wear out' the Protestants," says Rev. J. A. Wylie, "in preference to summarily exterminating them by fire and cord. It is true the murders in the fields were numerous; there were few spots in the Cevennes which martyr blood did not moisten; but only occasionally in the cities was the scaffold set up." *History of Protestantism*, Vol. III.

In the year 1700, the Duke de la Force obtained permission to march to Perigord at the head of several regiments, and this he desired to do in order to compel the Huguenots who lived in the royal towns of that province to embrace the Roman Catholic faith. He accordingly entered the town of Bergerac accompanied by four Jesuit[1] priests and escorted by a regiment of Dragoons, whom he quartered[2] among the citizens.

The inhuman conduct of these Dragoons proved more effective in inducing the Huguenots to forsake their religion than all the exhortations of the Jesuits had been. The most barbarous means were adopted to drive the unhappy citizens to the mass and to persuade them to abjure the Protestant faith. For this purpose a formulary[3] was drawn up, filled with imprecations[4] against the opinions of the Huguenots, which all the inhabitants of Bergerac were constrained to sign and confirm by oath.

At that time, there lived in the town a worthy citizen to whom I shall give the name of Mantel *(Martielhe)*. Engaged in trade, he conscientiously fulfilled the duties of his calling. As the father of a family, he educated his children in the fear of God, instructing them in the principles of true religion and, as the circumstances of the times indeed demanded, he sought to guard them against the errors of Popery. Twenty-two Dragoons

---

1. Priests of the Society of Jesus; the very arm of the Catholic Counter-Reformation. Ignatius Loyola (1491-1556), founder of that order and author of *"The Spiritual Exercises,"* states in that work, "To be right in everything, we ought always to hold that the white which I see, is black, if the Hierarchical Church so decides it."

2. Stationed and housed them among the citizens of the town.

3. A document containing prescribed forms for rituals, beliefs, and prayers.

4. A curse; an invocation of calamity or evil upon someone.

were quartered by the Duke in the house of this honest man, nor was this all, he himself was arrested and thrown into prison without regard to law or justice. Happily, his oldest son had previously effected his own escape, but two other sons and a daughter, still in early childhood, were taken from their home and placed in a convent.[1]

The unfortunate mother of this once happy family was then left alone, surrounded by two and twenty ruffians, who, having first treated her with the utmost barbarity and destroyed everything in the house so that nothing remained but the bare walls, afterwards dragged her into the presence of the duke where, by the basest treatment and the most terrible threats, she was at length compelled to sign the formulary. Weeping bitterly, the poor woman solemnly protested against these proceedings and determined publicly to state her objection, although she was yet obliged to put her name to the document. When the Duke, therefore, placed the formulary before her, she did indeed sign her name as she was commanded, but she added these words, "The Duke de la Force has compelled me to sign." The Duke insisted upon her scratching out this bold declaration, but she steadily refused until at length one of the Jesuits took a pen and effaced the offending sentence. But here we must leave the unhappy mother in order to follow the oldest son, now a fugitive, whose narrative of escape we will give in his own words.

---

1. According to an edict of Louis XIV, Protestant schools and churches were closed, pastors banished, and soldiers were quartered in Protestant households. All Protestant children were made to attend Roman Catholic schools and receive instruction in the Catholic catechism. All children over six, whose parents were suspected of remaining Protestant at heart, were removed from their homes and placed in the care of Catholic relatives, convents or asylums. Rev. J. A. Wylie, *History of Protestantism*, Vol. III.

CHAPTER 2
FLIGHT

CHAPTER 2
FLIGHT

fled from my father's house before the Dragoons entered. It was in October, 1700 that I left my home, being at that time about sixteen years of age. I was young indeed to be exposed to such perils, with scarcely sufficient prudence and experience to extricate myself from them. Could I hope to elude the vigilance of the soldiers who occupied all parts of the town? Nevertheless, by God's goodness, I was enabled to effect my escape. Accompanied by a young friend, I fled at night without being observed and, pursuing our journey through a forest, we found ourselves the next morning at Mussidan, a small town which lies about three leagues distant from Bergerac. From there we resolved, in spite of any obstacles that might arise, to continue our journey to Holland. We solemnly committed ourselves to the protection of God and resigned ourselves to his will in all the dangers that might await us. And we determined by his grace not to look back, as Lot's wife did,[1] but to abide steadfastly in the profession of the true faith, although we might be sentenced to death or to hard labor in the Galleys on account of that faith.

---

1. A reference to the story and the admonition: "But his wife looked back from behind him, and she became a pillar of salt," Genesis 19:26, and, "Remember Lot's wife. Whosoever shall seek to save his life shall lose it; and whosoever shall lose his life shall preserve it," Luke 17:32-33.

Thus, having called upon God for his grace and assistance, we set off cheerfully on the road to Paris. Our purse was not particularly well stocked, our whole property consisting only of ten pistoles[1] or about 20*s*. We endeavored to spend as little as possible of this small sum, and when we were obliged to purchase refreshments, we always turned into the poorest looking inn we could find. We met with no accident, thank God, until we arrived at Paris on November 10, 1700. In Paris, according to the plan we had proposed to follow on our departure from Bergerac, we sought out an acquaintance from whom we hoped to learn the easiest and safest way of reaching the frontier. We were very happy to obtain from a Protestant friend a written direction as far as Mezières, an out-post on the river Mêuse, which formed the boundary of the Spanish Netherlands and was adjoined to the Forest of Ardennes. This friend assured us that we had nothing to fear until we came to Mezières and that we might, upon leaving it, go through the Forest of Ardennes to Charleroi; Charleroi being only six miles distance from Mezières. If we could only succeed in reaching Charleroi, which was occupied by a Dutch garrison, we would be beyond the French frontier and consequently, we would be in perfect security. But he cautioned us, above all things, to be on our guard when passing through Mezières because all strangers that entered that town are subject to a strict examination and if any are found without a passport,[2] they are immediately thrown

---

1. A gold coin of Spain, but used in the neighboring countries also.

2. A passport in the early eighteenth century was not the same as that issued in modern times; it might have been issued for a whole party of persons and was a specific license from a king or authorized authority that granted a safe conduct for passage through a specific territory, that is, permission to travel or pass through a place without hindrance by any persons living there.

into prison. We accordingly set off on our journey from Paris to Mezières.

In the interior of France, travelers are allowed to pass without being questioned by the police; it is only in the frontier towns that they are strictly watched. We therefore proceeded quietly on our way until, at about five o'clock one afternoon, we came to the top of a hill from where we saw in front of us, about a quarter of a mile from the place where we stood, the town of Mezières and the gate by which we must enter that city. You may easily imagine what our feelings were as the danger that we were about to meet with was so suddenly brought before our eyes. We sat down there on the hill and considered how we might best gain entrance into the town. We saw that from the gate there extended a bridge over the river Mêuse, and that upon this bridge many of the citizens were walking and enjoying the fine weather.

The thought immediately suggested itself, "Let us mingle with the crowd and walk up and down on the bridge, so that, when the citizens return into the town, we might pass through the gate with the rest of them without exciting any observation." We immediately rose, took out the clothes that were in our knapsacks, dressed ourselves in them, and stuffed the knapsacks into the pockets of our coats. Then, rubbing the dust from our shoes and smoothing out our hair that we might not have the appearance of travelers, we went down the hill and, arriving at the bridge, we walked up and down with the citizens until the sound of the trumpet gave notice that the gates were about to be closed. The citizens hastened into the town and we followed in the throng and happily without being observed by the sentinel. We were truly glad to have escaped this danger, imagining then that it was the only one we had to fear. Truly, as will be seen in the sequel, we had not considered whoever might be our host that evening.

We could not possibly leave Mezières that night, as the gate on the opposite side of the town was locked and we were therefore obliged to seek a lodging. We entered the first inn we saw and here we were received by the good woman of the house, her husband being at that time absent. We ordered supper and about nine o'clock, just as we were sitting down to eat, the landlord returned. His wife informed him that during his absence she had admitted two young strangers. He asked her, loud enough for us to hear, whether we were provided with a passport from the Governor, to which she replied that she had not inquired. "What, foolish woman!" he continued, "do you wish to ruin us? You know the strict orders we have received not to let anyone remain in our house without permission. I must go directly with the strangers to the Governor."

Our uneasiness at hearing these words was great. Our landlord presently entered our apartment and inquired with much civility, whether we had seen the Governor. We replied that we had not, adding that we had not considered it necessary, since we only intended to remain in the town for one night. Upon hearing this, he told us that if the Governor knew of our being in his house without permission, he would be fined the amount of a thousand dollars. "But," he said, "have you a passport seeing that you venture thus into a frontier town?" In this perplexity, alas, we were tempted to be unfaithful to the truth and thus we replied to his question, apparently with perfect confidence, that we had a passport. "That makes the case different," responded our host, "I have then nothing to fear from receiving you into my house without permission. Nevertheless, you must accompany me to the Governor, in order that he may examine your passport." We objected, declaring that we were weary with our journey and that if he would wait until the next morning, we would then willingly follow him. To this he was persuaded to agree and we, having had our supper, lay down on the comfortable beds prepared for us. But, so completely were our minds occupied with the perils that surrounded us that we could not sleep.

How many plans did we form during this long night for escaping from the vigilance of the Governor, while our consciences smote us for our past dissimulation.[1] But, since no human help was near, we could finally only commit ourselves in this overwhelming trouble to Almighty God, imploring his assistance and praying that, if it was his will to test us, he would grant us the courage and steadfastness to make a worthy confession of the Evangelical faith. As soon as it was day, we rose and went into the kitchen. Previously, while we were dressing, a means of escape had occurred to us, namely, to leave the house if possible, unperceived by the host and before he had time to observe[2] us more closely. He slept in a room adjoining the kitchen, and hearing us there, he inquired what we wanted so early in the morning.

We replied that we wished to have breakfast before we went to the Governor's, in order that we might continue our journey as soon as we had spoken to the Governor. He approved our plan and desired the servant to prepare our breakfast while he rose and dressed himself.

---

1. Concealing of some fact, in this case, their intentions and identities.
2. To take account of.

We observed, however, that the maid had forgotten to shut the kitchen door that opened into the street: thus we went out without our host suspecting anything. No sooner were we in the street than, having asked a little boy which was the way to the gate that led to Charleville, we proceeded towards it and thus escaped the fatal inn without taking leave of those who dwelt there. The gate was not very distant and, passing through it without inquiry, we went on to Charleville. Charleville is a little town within reach of gunshot from Mezières and which has neither gates nor a garrison. Here we had a hearty breakfast and then, continuing on our journey, we left Charleville and entered the Forest of Ardennes.

There had been a hard frost during the night and the trees were covered with icicles. When we had proceeded some distance through the woods, we arrived at a place where a number of roads met and we were completely at a loss which road we should take. While we were considering this, a peasant came up to us and we immediately requested that he show us the road to Charleroi. He answered, at the same time shrugging his shoulders significantly, that he saw that we must be strangers by our proposing to go to Charleroi through the forest, which was a thing impossible for anyone not perfectly acquainted with the road, since there were so many paths crossing each other throughout the woods, and not a village or even a cottage any place near; and, he continued, that if we attempted to find our own way, we would only get deeper into the woods and probably either fall prey to the wolves which abounded there or perish with cold and hunger. We offered the peasant a louis d'or[1] if he would guide us through the forest to

1. A gold coin.

Charleroi. "No," he said, "not if you would give me a hundred louis d'ors. I am sure that you are Huguenots and have fled from your homes, and to render you such a service would be to fasten the halter[1] on my own neck. But I will give you this advice: leave the Forest of Ardennes and take the road to your right, which will lead you to a village where you may find a lodging for the night and tomorrow you can proceed on your journey. Still keeping to the right and leaving Rocroy to the left, you will come to the small town of Couvé through which you must pass. When you leave it, turn down a road to the left, which will lead you to Charleroi. The distance is certainly greater than travelling through the Forest of Ardennes, but it is much safer." We thanked the honest man and followed his directions.

We arrived at the village he mentioned, where we remained the night. Early the next morning, we proceeded on our journey, leaving Rocroy to the left. But the peasant, probably from ignorance, had omitted to warn us that the road led through a narrow pass that was guarded by a French sentinel, who was under strict orders to arrest all persons travelling without a passport and to take them prisoners to Rocroy.

Like wandering sheep, we strayed into the lion's den. Nevertheless, by the good providence of God, we escaped the impending danger. For, as we entered the narrow pass, there began so heavy a shower of rain to fall that the sentinel ran for shelter into the guard house, and thus we passed by without exciting his observation. Shortly after, we arrived at Couvé where we might have remained in perfect security had we known that this little town was beyond the French frontier. It belonged

---

1. A rope for hanging malefactors.

to the Prince of Liege, and it was within gunshot of Liege, which was manned by a Dutch garrison and the Governor was accustomed to grant an escort to all fugitives who wished to go to Charleroi.

But of this we were not aware and God allowed us to remain in ignorance, in order to test our faith by the experience of the greatest misery.

CHAPTER 3
IMPRISONMENT

CHAPTER 3
IMPRISONMENT

aving eluded the vigilance of the sentinel at the entrance to Couvé, we proceeded immediately to the inn in order to dry our clothes, which were thoroughly soaked by the rain, and to obtain some refreshments. Here a very trying circumstance was the cause of all our subsequent misfortunes. Having ordered some beer, it was brought to us in a can[1] and, on our requesting that the landlord bring glasses, our host remarked that he perceived that we must be Frenchmen or we might have been contented to have drunk from the can according to the customs of the country.

There were several persons in the room when the landlord spoke and, among others, an inhabitant of the town and a ranger in the service of the Prince of Liege. This latter took upon himself to examine us and, sitting down beside us, he began by saying, "I will lay a wager that you have no rosary with you." My companion happened to be grating snuff at the time and, holding up his grater, thoughtlessly replied, "Here is my rosary." This confirmed the ranger in his opinion that we were Protestants and he immediately formed the resolution of betraying us. Meanwhile, suspecting nothing, we left Couvé and, following the directions of the peasant,

---

1. A pitcher made of metal.

took the road to the left. But we had not walked far before we perceived a man on horseback—who, from his appearance, we judged to be an officer—coming to meet us. Alarmed lest he might prove to be an enemy, we retraced our steps and turned down the road that led to Marienburg.

Marienburg is a very small town and has only one gate. We ought to have pursued our journey to Charleroi, but as the evening was far advanced, we thought it better to remain for the night at an inn opposite the gate. Here we found a comfortable lodging and hoped to obtain some hours' repose. But we had not been there more than half an hour when a man entered the room and with much civility inquired where we came from and where we were going. Supposing him to be the landlord, we replied that we came from Paris and were on our way to Philippeville. "I must inform the Governor of your arrival," he continued. We tried to put him off as we had done the landlord at Mezières, but to no avail, for he commanded us in a haughty tone to follow him immediately. Notwithstanding this unexpected misfortune, we were not discouraged and we rose to accompany him with apparent indifference. I said to my companion in our own language, which the stranger did not understand, that as the night was so dark, we might possibly escape on our way to the Governor's. But this we soon found would be impossible, for in the court stood eight soldiers with fixed bayonets and at their head was the treacherous ranger from Couvé, who was himself the cause of our arrest. We proceeded to the Governor's house and were conducted into his presence. He demanded of us where we were coming from and what our destination was. To the first question we answered truly, but to the second we replied that we were barbers and were on our way to Philippeville from where it was our intention to visit Maubeuge, Valenciennes, Cambray, and other places, and then to return to our native town.

The Governor, in order to convince himself of the truth of our statement, desired that one of his servants, who was a barber by trade, examine what proficiency we had made in the art. He happily turned his questions to my companion, who had learned that business, and whose answers appeared to satisfy the Governor. The Governor then further inquired, "What religion do you profess?" To this we openly replied that we were attached to the Reformed religion, for on this most solemn subject we would have been ashamed to be unfaithful to the truth. Would to God that we had answered with equal sincerity,[1] the other questions which the Governor put to us, for, as I have learned by painful experience, one must carefully shun the ways of falsehood in order to keep the conscience clear and maintain a firm confidence in God, and in order to avoid stumbling on a slippery path. But, alas, how prone is the human heart to depart from uprightness! How easily is it led into a snare, being led away by fear or numerous other motives to deny the truth, even when it has the clearest apprehension of that which is right and the most sincere desire to practice it! And having once been led into sin, it falls naturally from one transgression to another, until it is brought into bondage and finds it impossible to escape. I look back, with deep and painful repentance, upon these deviations from the path of rectitude.

When the Governor charged us with the intention of leaving the kingdom, we most strongly denied ever having formed such a resolution.

---

1. Honesty and truthfulness.

The examination lasted an hour, after which the Governor commanded the Major of the garrison to see us lodged safely in the public prison. On the way there, the major, M. de la Salle, asked me whether it was true that I was a native of Bergerac, and when I declared positively that this was the case, he continued, "I myself was born there and formerly lived about a mile from that town. What is your name?" "Mantel *(Martielhe),*" I replied. "Indeed!" he exclaimed, "your father, then, is one of my earliest friends. Be comforted, my children, I shall do everything in my power to deliver you from your unfortunate situation, and I trust in two or three days to be able to restore you to liberty."

While he spoke, we arrived at the prison, which, at the sight of its gloomy walls, we were overwhelmed with anguish. "Alas!" we asked with tears, "What crime have we committed that we should be treated as criminals worthy of the severest punishment?" "My children," answered the major compassionately, "I must obey orders, but, if it is possible, I will prevent your remaining all night in this detestable place." He left us and went directly to the Governor, whom he informed that, having searched our persons and found us in possession of nothing but a five dollar piece, he was fully convinced that we had never meditated an escape from France and that he thought it was only just to set us at liberty. Unfortunately, the post[1] for Paris had been dispatched that evening and in it the Governor had written to inform the court of our arrest. It was therefore no longer in his power to dismiss us. At the Major's earnest entreaty, however, he permitted us to leave the dungeon and take up our abode in the jailer's

---

1. Mail.

house, our kind benefactor pledging his word that we would not escape.

In about half an hour, the Major returned to the prison, accompanied by a corporal and private of the guard, and informed us that he had obtained permission for us to lodge in an apartment in the jailer's house. It was this jailer into whose care he had entrusted the money we had previously given up to him, saying that, so long as it lasted, it was to be used for our support. The kindness of the Major softened, in some degree, the sad intelligence he brought us from the Governor, as to the possibility of our release.

Shortly afterwards, a very favorable representation of our case was sent to the court at Paris, but our confession of the Protestant faith so irritated the Minister of State, the Marquis de la Brillière, that he thought no other part of the letter was worthy of his attention and he dispatched immediate orders to the Governor of Marienburg that we, being convicted of having passed the boundary without a passport, should without further delay be sentenced to the Galleys. Before the sentence was to be carried into execution, however, the priest at Marienburg was to do all in his power to persuade us to enter the Romish Church, so that if he succeeded in converting us to the "true" faith, we might obtain a free pardon, be set at liberty, and be sent back to Bergerac. The Major himself read this letter to us, remarking, when he had finished it, "Do not expect me to advise you as to your future conduct; your consciences alone must decide. All I can say is this: in renouncing the Protestant doctrines, you will open the doors of your prison; and to abide in them, will inevitably lead you to the Galleys." We answered him thus: "We have placed our whole confidence in God, and we humbly submit ourselves to his good pleasure. Human help we do not expect; but by the grace of Him, upon whom we continually call for support, we will never deny the Reformed faith or renounce the divine principles of our holy religion. Do not suppose our decision proceeds from obstinacy or self-will. We thank God it is from knowledge and a firm conviction of the truth of those tenets which our parents took so much pain to teach us and which, contrary to the errors of the Romish Church, we remain constant in our adherence to the Protestant faith." We then warmly thanked the Major for the exertions he had made on our behalf, assuring him that, although we had no means of openly testifying of our gratitude, he would daily be remembered in our prayers. Our kind friend embraced us with fatherly affection, declaring he felt as deeply on the subject as we ourselves did, and then he hurried away to conceal his emotions. I truly believe that he was at heart a Protestant and only externally conformed to the rites of the Roman Catholic Church.

Meanwhile our money was nearly spent and we received only a pound and a half of bread daily from the jailer. But, as we were alternately furnished with provisions by the Governor and our friend the Major and, by the kindness of the chief ecclesiastic as well as the monks, were also liberally supplied, we were able even to contribute to the maintenance of the jailer and his family.

The confessor visited us almost daily and put into our hands a Romish catechism, which we compared with the catechism of Drelincourt that we had with us. The priest gave us permission to dispute with him either from tradition or from the Holy Scriptures, but when we chose the latter, he was not well pleased and dropped the subject altogether after two or three conversations. Finding that all his endeavors to win us by the prospect of temporal advantage were fruitless, the priest declared to both the Governor and the recorder that, since we obstinately rendered all arguments unavailing, he could hold out no hope for our conversion. Upon hearing this, it was resolved to pronounce our sentence. The recorder and his clerk came to the prison and commenced a judicial examination. Two days afterwards, we heard our sentence, which ran as follows: "That having been convicted of endeavoring to escape the kingdom contrary to the command of the King, of passing the boundary without a passport and, above all, of being, according to our own confession, Protestants, we were sentenced to hard labor in the Galleys for life."

The recorder asked whether we would appeal to the high court at Tournay. We replied that, since all men were against us, we desired to appeal from this unjust sentence to the judgment seat of God. "I beg of you," he continued, "not to ascribe the extreme severity of your punishment to me. No, believe me, it is by command of the King that you are condemned, but, since you will not appeal for yourselves, my duty requires that I should appeal to the Parliament in your names. Prepare yourselves, therefore, to go to Tournay." "We are prepared for everything," was our reply.

CHAPTER 4
SECOND
IMPRISONMENT

CHAPTER 4
SECOND
IMPRISONMENT

e were not again permitted to leave our prison until we commenced our journey to Tournay. We made the journey on foot, guarded by four constables, our arms bound with a cord by which also we were fastened together. In this disgraceful manner, we passed through Philippeville, Maubeuge, and Valenciennes. In the evening, when we had finished our day's march, we were thrown into a loathsome prison where we were obliged to lie upon the hard ground without even a little straw to cover us and bread and water being the only food allowed to us. Thus we were treated like the most vile criminals, worthy of the most ignominious[1] punishments. When we arrived at Tournay, we were placed in the Parliamentary prison. We had not a farthing of money left and being given only a pound and a half of bread daily and no longer supplied by the bounty of charitable persons, we expected to be almost starved to death.

To increase our distress, the priest prevailed upon the Parliament to delay our trial until he should, as he said, succeed in converting us to the "true" faith. But—whether from indolence, or from the hope of

---

1. Disgraceful.

overcoming our resolution, by making us suffer the pangs of hunger, I do not know—he never visited us more than once a week and sometimes only once in the fortnight,[1] and then he spoke so little upon the subject of religion that we had no opportunity of defending ourselves. On one occasion, when we endeavored to express our opinions, he interrupted us saying, "Another time," and immediately left the prison. Meanwhile we became so thin and weak that we could scarcely hold ourselves upright. A little damp straw full of vermin was our only couch, and yet even on this we were glad to rest. And happily it was near the door or we would never have been able to reach our food, which was thrown to us as if we were dogs. In this extreme misery, we sold our coats and waistcoats to the turnkey[2] for a little bread. And indeed, shortly after, we sold all our clothes except the clothes we had on our backs, but alas, these soon became old and tattered.

No one visited us but the priest, whose only question was whether we were not weary of enduring so much misery. To this he added that no mercy would be shown to us because our freedom depended upon us alone. In order to obtain liberty, we only had to renounce the errors of Calvin. His language at last grew so harsh and offensive that we gave him no further reply.

We had been about six weeks in this distressing situation, when early one morning the turnkey threw a broom into the dungeon and commanded us to make haste immediately to sweep it clean, as they were going to bring two young noblemen to keep us company. We asked what crime they were accused of. "Of being Huguenots, like yourselves," he answered.

---

1. A period of fourteen days; two weeks.
2. The jailer who keeps the keys.

Imprisonment in the loathsome
prison at Tourney.

In a quarter of an hour, the doors of our prison were again thrown open and the jailer entered, followed by several soldiers, who conducted two young and richly appareled gentlemen. And having seen them safely lodged and the doors locked, the whole party retired. As soon as they were gone, we went up to salute our companions. We had immediately recognized them to be two of our former schoolfellows, the sons of respectable citizens in Bergerac. I shall speak of the one as Salmon and of the other as Roubert, but the former gave himself out as being the Chevalier de Salmon and the other called himself the Marquis de Roubert, hoping that if they assumed these titles they would be able the more easily to effect their escape from France.

They were astonished beyond measure when we addressed them by their names for, as emaciated as we were from our sufferings, they did not recognize us. Nor was their surprise diminished when we made ourselves known to them. They told us that our relations and friends had long mourned our loss, for not having heard of us for the last six months or more, they supposed that we had either fallen prey to sickness or had been murdered on our journey. The fact was that during our captivity we were not allowed to write to anyone. After this explanation, we heartily embraced and together bewailed our sad fate.

Our fellow-prisoners then inquired if we had anything for them to eat, as they were very hungry. We gave them our portion of bread to which they exclaimed, "Is this the way they mean to treat us likewise? And will not even money purchase a little food?" "Oh yes," we replied, "if you are supplied with money, you will do well enough; but our misfortune is that for the last three months we have had no money at all." "Oh," they said, "if money will purchase what we want, we have plenty." And with that, they pulled out of their pockets and shoes, where they had concealed it, gold to the amount of four hundred louis d'ors. We felt unspeakable pleasure at the sight of this treasure; for now we might hope for some relief from the intolerable pangs of hunger, which we daily suffered for want of sufficient food. They put into my hand a five dollar piece and begged me to order a good supply of provisions immediately. I was not slow to obey, and my loud calls soon summoned the turnkey. I gave him the five dollar piece, desiring him to bring us something to eat as soon as possible. "Very well, gentlemen," he replied; "what will you have? Some soup and boiled meat?" "Yes, yes," I said, "and plenty of bread and beer." "I will return with your dinner in an hour," he answered, as he left the prison. "An hour!" I exclaimed. "Oh what a long time to wait!" The newcomers could not help laughing at my impatience, but they had eaten a hearty meal not many hours before and had not experienced the pangs of hunger.

At last the turnkey returned, bringing with him so abundant a supply of provisions that I really believe a dozen hungry men would have found enough to satisfy their appetites. As for my companion and me, we ate so heartily that, reduced as we were by long fasting, a severe fit of indigestion was the consequence of our imprudence.

After our repast,[1] our friends inquired by what unfortunate circumstances we had been reduced to so miserable a condition, upon which we gave an exact account of all that had befallen us since our departure from Bergerac. When we had concluded, they replied by lamenting their own weakness and confessing that

---

1. Meal.

they had not the courage to adopt so decided a line of conduct as we had done, but that they had resolved rather to renounce their religion than to submit to the disgrace of being sentenced to the Galleys. "What!" I exclaimed, "Would you set us such an example? Better, far better for us that we had never seen you than that we should have to witness your departure from the faith! A step so opposed to the education you have received, and to the knowledge of those truths in which you have been instructed! Do you not fear the righteous judgment of God? Does he not say that those who know his will and do not do it shall be beaten with many more stripes than those who do not know it? Can there be a more awful warning?" They answered, "We cannot possibly submit to becoming slaves in the Galleys. You are very happy in having firmness to endure this ignominious punishment and we commend your constancy, but let us say no more upon the subject, as our resolution is firm and we shall not change it." We could only lament their weakness and pray that God in his mercy would deliver them from their errors.

Two days after this conversation, they were summoned before the Parliament, quickly examined, and finally asked whether they would consent to embrace the Roman Catholic religion. They replied that it was their earnest desire to do so. "Well," returned the president, "you shall have the necessary instruction previous to the public abjuration of your Protestant errors, and after that, we will immediately proceed to your liberation." They were, in the mean time, sent back to prison, where they arrived in high spirits. But we could not sympathize with their joy, as we felt the greatest detestation of their apostasy.

In the course of a few hours after their examination before the Parliament, they were visited by the priest who bestowed upon them the highest praises for their conduct and put into their hands a catechism, which he desired them to learn, as their deliverance depended on their making themselves thoroughly acquainted with it. The young men accordingly studied day and night, but on the third evening all their hopes of freedom were unfortunately dispelled by the arrival of two messengers, who had come to conduct them before the Parliament. There they were taken with their hands bound like criminals. The president addressed them thus: "Gentlemen, it is now three days since we promised to set you at liberty on condition of your renouncing the Protestant faith. We do not wish to deceive you and, therefore, think that it is right to tell you that it is no longer in our power to fulfill that promise. We have received a letter from the court in which we have positive orders to proceed against you according to the severity of that law which prohibits any French subject from quitting[1] the kingdom. By command of the King, you are sentenced to the Galleys. You may now, gentlemen, renounce your religion, if you please. Such a noble step would be commendable in the highest degree, but we repeat, it will not now procure your freedom." They answered that in this case, they would prefer adhering to the Reformed doctrines. "Excellent Catholics!" exclaimed the president, and remanded them to prison. They were now as much bowed down with shame and grief, as they had been formerly elated by hope, and they constantly lamented their sad destiny with tears. In less than a week, their sentence was read to them, which declared that they were condemned to labor in the Galleys for life.

---

1. Escaping; leaving.

The day after this sentence was passed against them, they were conducted to Lisle on foot by four constables. The people thronged the streets to see them pass, believing that they belonged to one of the first families in France, as they had assumed the titles of nobility. At Lisle, they were visited by the Jesuits, who at last persuaded them openly to profess the Catholic religion. And this they did by promising to use every means in their power to obtain their liberty, which, after many fruitless exertions, they did actually accomplish through the influence of Madame de Maintenon.[1] Madame de Maintenon not only procured this favor for them but further got them commissions in one of the French regiments. We heard afterwards that they both perished in a battle against the Huguenots.

I have already related that assistance they had given us in our great distress for food. Knowing that they had plenty of money and fearing that we should again suffer from hunger, I was inclined to ask them to lend me three or four louis d'ors, which I promised them should be paid back to them from Bergerac. But my request was in vain. Little touched by our misery, they would only leave us half a louis d'or and this I returned to them shortly after when we met in the prison at Lisle. This was a few days before they were set at liberty. In the mean time, we lived as frugally as possible and never tasted anything but bread.

I have mentioned that the Parliamentary Confessor[2] occasionally visited us, not for the purpose of convincing us of our errors by sound and rational arguments, but to

---

1. See the *Historical Background* for information regarding Madame de Maintenon.
2. The priest.

see whether continued privation[1] would not reduce us to submission. About this time, the Bishop of Tournay, hearing of our condition, sent his Chaplain to instruct us. He was a good old man, but little acquainted with controversy. He told us that he came by order of the Bishop to convert us to the Christian faith. We replied that we were already Christians by baptism and by our belief in the Gospel of Jesus Christ. "What!" he exclaimed with surprise, "Are you Christians?" Supposing he had made some mistake, he asked our names and looked at his tablets to ascertain that we were the persons to whom he had been sent. We told him our Christian and surnames. "You are certainly the persons that the Bishop desired me to visit," he replied. "Let me hear you repeat the articles of your faith." We answered him by saying the Apostles' Creed. "Do you believe in that?" he inquired. And when we assured him that we firmly believed in the doctrines it contains, he declared with some displeasure that the Bishop must have wished to make a fool of him—*it being the 1st of April, 1701*—and added that a man of his age and character ought not to have been trifled with in such a manner. He then nastily left us.

The next morning the Bishop sent his grand Vicar, Mr. Regnier, to see us. Mr. Regnier was a very intelligent, kind-hearted man and one who was better acquainted with theology than the good old Chaplain. Finding us well grounded in the articles of the Protestant faith and firmly persuaded of the errors of the Romish Church, he was the more desirous of effecting our conversion to the Catholic religion. He visited us daily and though we never could agree on the subject of religion, since

---

1. To be deprived of those things that are necessary.

he held fast to tradition and we to the Holy Scriptures,[1] yet he took every opportunity of showing us kindness. Seeing that we were greatly in want of clothes, he left a supply of clothing for us at the prison, particularly desiring that we should not be told where it came from. And with the Bishop's permission, during Passion Week, having given each of the prisoners six groshen, he presented us, in the prelate's name, with four louis d'ors. At first we refused to accept them, but on his representing to us that the Bishop would impute[2] our reluctance to pride, we accepted his kindness with gratitude. Indeed, we found his present most useful, for we were greatly distressed for lack of money to purchase the necessities of life.

The Confessor of the Parliament was displeased at the grand Vicar's exertions in our behalf. He disputed the Vicar's right to visit the prison, saying that the prison did not belong to the jurisdiction of the Bishop. By the prelate's influence, therefore, we were transferred to the state prison. In the state prison we were far more comfortable than before. Many respectable Protestant citizens at Tournay obtained permission to see us and with large presents of money they induced the jailer to allow us to pass a few hours every morning in the court in front of the house. Here our faithful friends often visited us, supporting us with their counsel and exhorting us to remain steadfast in the faith. The grand

---

1. The Roman Catholic religion is founded upon a development of doctrine through tradition, while Protestantism is firmly grounded in that original Gospel, even as it was preached from the beginning. "I marvel," says the Apostle, "that ye are so soon removed from him that called you into the grace of Christ unto another Gospel: which is not another; but there be some that trouble you, and would pervert the Gospel of Christ. But though we, or an angel from heaven, preach any other Gospel unto you than that which we have preached unto you, let him be accursed," Galatians 1:6-8.

2. Attribute or account.

Vicar found them with us several times and, far from being displeased, begged them to remain and listen to our conversation. The argument which followed often lasted for a couple of hours and at its conclusion the Vicar would send for wine and insist upon our drinking to each other's health before we parted. At last, finding that we could not agree upon the subject in dispute, he proposed a compromise. "You are at liberty," he said, "to reject the invocation of the Virgin Mary, the worship of images, the adoration of the saints, purgatory, indulgences, and pilgrimages, if you will believe in transubstantiation[1] and the sacrifice of the mass,[2] and agree to renounce the errors of Calvin." We assured him that our consciences would never allow us to renounce any of the doctrines of the Protestant faith.

1. The Catholic belief that the bread and wine of communion are changed by the priest into the real body and blood of Jesus Christ in order that he may be sacrificed afresh at the mass. This novel doctrine originates in the scholastic era of the high middle ages, the controversy itself began among Catholic theologians only as early as the 9th century, and the dogma was not settled among them until the 13th century. Jesus showed in the Gospel that he was not to be eaten as men eat food (John 6:58), but in the spirit alone: "It is the spirit that quickens; the flesh profits nothing: the words that I speak unto you, they are spirit, and they are life," John 6:63.

2. The doctrine that the mass is the actual and real offering up of Jesus Christ for sin. This doctrine goes against the Gospel which teaches that Jesus Christ was offered up once for all time, his death being sufficient for all the sins of the world: "For such an high priest became us, who is holy, harmless, undefiled, separate from sinners, and made higher than the heavens; who needs not daily, as those high priests, to offer up sacrifice, first for his own sins, and then for the people's: for this he did once, when he offered up himself," Hebrews 7:26-27; and again, "But Christ being come an high priest of good things to come, by a greater and more perfect tabernacle, not made with hands, that is to say, not of this building; neither by the blood of goats and calves, but by his own blood he entered in once *(ephapax, once for all)* into the holy place, having obtained eternal redemption for us," Hebrews 9:11-12; and yet again, "So Christ was once *(hapax, once for all)* offered to bear the sins of many," Hebrews 9:28. The Catholic doctrine has Jesus Christ appearing in the flesh at every mass that he might continually offer himself in sacrifice for sin.

From that time his visits became less frequent and soon ceased altogether. But we had reason to believe that his kind feelings toward us continued, for a few days afterwards a Member of Parliament called at the prison and informed us that we in particular had been recommended to his attention, adding that he came to make himself more exactly acquainted with the specifics of our case. We could only suppose that our kind friend, the grand Vicar, had spoken to this gentleman, as we knew no one else from whom the recommendation could likely have come from. The member remained an hour with us and asked many questions beginning with which road we had taken from Bergerac and what had befallen us on our journey. We gave him an accurate account of all that had happened since we left our homes. He listened attentively until we mentioned our unfortunate visit to Couvé, and then he interrupted us by asking whether or not we could prove that we had been in an inn in that town. We answered that nothing could be easier for us to do. "Well then, my young friends," he continued, "if this is the case, I can encourage you to hope that your affairs may yet have a happy end. I will send a lawyer tomorrow morning, who will draw up a petition, which you must sign. And I trust you will experience the advantage of following my advice."

Here he left us and the very next morning a lawyer brought the petition for our signatures. The petition was as follows:

"That though we were Protestants, we had not made ourselves obnoxious to those punishments denounced in the royal edict against fugitives, because we could prove that we never had any intention of escaping from France. It was evident that after we had quitted the kingdom we had voluntarily returned to it, since we had been in Couvé, a city belonging to the Prince of Liege and defended by a Dutch garrison. We had clearly only intended to pass through this city, taking this road by Rocroy to Marienburg. If we had really wished to leave France, we would have put ourselves under the protection of the Governor of Couvé, who without difficulty could have sent us through the bishopric of Liege to Charleroi."

As this petition was founded upon falsehood, how could we expect a blessing to accompany it? And it was the merited punishment of our dishonesty that the newly awakened light of hope was once more extinguished. Two days after this, we were summoned before the Parliament. The president told us that he had read our petition and saw that we wished to prove that we had passed through Couvé. "But," he continued, "can you also prove that at the time you were in Couvé you knew that this city lay beyond the frontier of France?" We had not expected to be asked this question, but we answered confidently, against our own consciences, that we were perfectly acquainted with the fact. "How could you know this?" he replied. "You are young and it is probable that you have never before been away from your homes, which are more than two hundred miles distance from Couvé." I did not know what reply to make to him, but my companion, Daniel le Gras, assured him that he was quite aware of it before his departure from Bergerac, adding that he "had served as a surgeon in one of the regiments from Picardy and that, at the time of the Peace of Ryswick, he was quartered[1] at Rocroy," from which place his regiment removed to Strasburg. And that it was in the latter city of Strasburg that he himself became a convert to the Reformed religion. How easy

---

1. Lodged.

would it have been for him at that time, he added, to have escaped from France and to have taken refuge in Holland or Germany! "If you are out of the service," remarked the president, "you must be in possession of a letter of discharge." Happily, Daniel had it with him and he presented it to the president, who caused it to be read aloud. The clerk of the court then fastened it to the petition and we were sent back to the prison.

Here I must observe[1] that Daniel le Gras had really been a surgeon in the regiment of Picardy and, after the Peace of Ryswick, had joined the Reformed Church of Strasburg. But he had never been at Rocroy and had merely invented this part of his story in his own defense. He left it to the Parliament to find out whether this regiment had been quartered at Rocroy or not. Thus, when we are tempted to leave the paths of uprightness, we become more and more entangled in the snare, like a man who, falling into a miry pit, sinks deeper and deeper in spite of all his efforts to get out. The falsehood was, however, not detected by the Member of Parliament who had so kindly interested himself on our behalf and who had secured many votes in our favor. Indeed, most of the deputies exerted themselves to obtain our freedom.

Two hours after our return to prison, the jailer hastened in to wish us joy of our approaching deliverance, for one of the ecclesiastics had told him that he had himself seen the decree which declared us completely innocent of the charge laid against us, namely, of wishing to quit[2] the kingdom. All of our friends in the town visited us and offered us many hearty congratulations on our good prospects, and we ourselves waited with

---

1. Remark.
2. Leave or escape.

much impatience for the happy moment that was to set us at liberty. But, alas, how soon were all our fair hopes blasted! The Parliament had indeed pronounced us innocent, but, as we were looked upon as prisoners of the state, we could not be dismissed without the permission of the court. The Attorney-General wrote word, therefore, to the Minister of State, the Marquis de la Brillière, at Paris, that we had satisfactorily proved our innocence and that the Parliament awaited his orders. The Minister replied that they ought to examine the case more fully to ensure that there was no deception. Not choosing to contradict their former statement, the Parliament replied that the proofs were sufficient and incontestable. A fortnight passed before any further communication was received from the court. At length the expected letter arrived and we were no longer in suspense as to our future fate. We were once more summoned before the Parliament. There we were asked by the president whether we could read, to which our answer was in the affirmative that we could. "Then read this letter," he replied, "which we have received from the Marquis de la Brillière." It was as follows:

Gentlemen,

John Mantel *(Jean Martielhe)* and Daniel le Gras have confessed that they passed the frontier without a passport; they are, therefore, sentenced to the Galleys by the express command of the King.

I am gentlemen, etc. etc.,
Marquis de la Brillière

"You see," added the president, "that this sentence proceeds not from us, but from the court of Paris. We are innocent of it and pity you most sincerely. We commend you to the mercy of God and the King."

CHAPTER 5
THIRD CAPTIVITY

CHAPTER 5
THIRD CAPTIVITY

hile the traveler, at every stage of his journey, meets with an inn that offers him refreshments and repose, we, during our wearisome and tedious march, found no lodging better than a gloomy prison and each dungeon we visited appeared more loathsome than the last.

Three days after we had received our final sentence we were sent on foot a distance of five miles to Lisle under the custody of four constables. Encumbered as we were with chains, we arrived there in the evening almost exhausted with fatigue. We were conducted to Peter's Tower. Peter's Tower was set apart, on account of its great strength, for the reception of the worst criminals. The jailer examined us closely and two Jesuits that were present took away our books, which were never again restored to us.

The prison at Lisle is large and spacious, but not a ray of light enters to cheer its unhappy inmates. Thus, the prisoners are only conscious of the returning day by the timing of the visits from their jailer. Every morning, the jailer brings in their scanty supply of bread and water. Their only bed consists of a little straw, half eaten by the rats and mice. The rats and mice also attack the food and devour it with impunity,[1] the light not being sufficient to allow them to be seen by the prisoners, who are thus unable to chase them away.

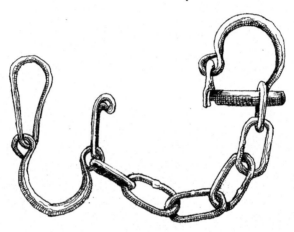

In this dreadful abode we were placed. Our companions were thirty profligates,[2] who were condemned to suffer the just punishment of their crimes. I could not distinguish any of them, but I heard their names called out by the jailer. A few days after our arrival at Lisle, the jailer offered me and my companion a room where we would be provided with a good bed and every other convenience on the condition that we could pay him two louis d'ors per month. We had very little money left, yet I offered him a louis d'or and a half if he would agree to board us until we were sent to the Galleys. This he refused, but he found reason afterwards to repent his decision.

About nine o'clock one morning, we heard our prison door open and ourselves being called by name. I thought our jailer had changed his mind and intended to remove

1. Without punishment.
2. Those who are lost to all sense of decency and morality.

us from there to a better room, but we were as happily astonished as a fisherman when he thinks he has caught a groundling and finds a carp in his net. Our jailer informed us that Baron von Lamberti, Chief Justice of Flanders and Governor of Lisle, wished to speak to us. We followed him to an apartment, where we found the Baron, who received us with kindness. He held in his hand a letter from his brother, a worthy Protestant nobleman, who lived only three miles from my native home of Bergerac, and who, at my father's request, had written to recommend us to the protection of the Baron. "I am sincerely grieved," he said to me, "that it is not in my power to procure your pardon. On behalf of any other criminal, I have sufficient influence at court to obtain such a request, but no one will venture to speak in favor of a Protestant. All that I can do therefore is to alleviate, in some degree, your sufferings and to keep you here as long as I please, even though the rest of the convicts must shortly be sent to the Galleys. Turning to the jailer, he asked whether there was a good room vacant. The jailer replied that there was and two or three were mentioned, but not thinking any sufficiently comfortable, he continued, "Well, then, it is my desire that you should at once remove them to the almonry[1] and see that they are allowed everything which might contribute to their comfort and help them to recover their strength." "Sir," interrupted the jailer, "that room is set apart for those prisoners who are allowed certain privileges not permitted to the others." "Well then," answered the Baron, "let these gentlemen be admitted to a share in those privileges. It is the duty of you and your assistants to see that they do not escape. And I repeat that they are to be allowed every convenience, but do not take any money from them. I wish all

---

1. The place where the almoner resides and the alms are distributed.

their expenses to be put on my account." "You will find," he added, addressing me, "this apartment more commodious than any in the prison." He also desired the jailer to make me superintendent of the room and distributor of the alms. We thanked him sincerely for his kindness and he, having promised to inquire often about our welfare, dismissed us.

The room in which we were now placed was large and comfortable. It contained six beds and was occupied by twelve prisoners including ourselves. The inmates here were often persons of high rank, but never those belonging to the lower classes. A few young boys, imprisoned for small frauds or other petty delinquencies, were employed to make our beds, sweep the room, cook our dinners, and do other menial offices. They slept on some straw at one end of the apartment. The office that I was appointed to fill was a very laborious one, namely, to distribute all the alms given to the prisoners. These generally amounted to a considerable sum, which was brought to me daily to be divided. The poor-box hung from one of the windows of the building, in order that the passers-by might be induced to contribute. This box, of which I kept the key, was opened every evening and a distribution made among those in my apartment, if they stood in need of such assistance, and also among the other criminals. The jailer always gave me a list of their names and, during the time I was at Lisle, their number amounted to between five and six hundred persons.

With all my exertions, I could not check a certain abuse, which had become too deeply rooted to be easily removed. It was this: the jailer, who daily received a certain sum from the poor-box to purchase food for the other prisoners, instead of spending it all for this purpose, generally furnished them with an ill-cooked mess of meat boiled with a little salt, the very smell of which was quite sufficient to make one ill. Thus, the poor inmates were deprived of the greater part of those gifts that were bestowed for their relief.

After we had spent six weeks in this apartment, Baron von Lamberti brought us information that the next day was fixed for the departure of the convicts to Dunkirk. "At Dunkirk," he continued, "there are stationed at present six Royal Galleys. However, I will exempt you from accompanying them by representing that you are ill and not able to walk. You must take to your beds and remain there until after the party has set out for Dunkirk." We did so and we found it much to our advantage that we were permitted to remain three months longer in the prison at Lisle.

CHAPTER 6
THE GALLEYS AT DUNKIRK

CHAPTER 6
THE GALLEYS AT DUNKIRK

n January, 1702, we received another visit from the Chief Justice, who told us that a party of criminals was to set off the next morning for Dunkirk and that he left us at liberty to accompany them or to remain longer in our present abode. But he added that this would be the last opportunity we would have of going to Dunkirk, as the next convoy would be to Marseilles. The distance to Marseilles being more than three hundred miles from Lisle, a journey that would be both difficult and painful for us to undertake, as we would be obliged to travel on foot and encumbered by heavy chains. Besides, he himself intended to leave Lisle in March, after which he could no longer be of any assistance to us there. "I strongly advise you, therefore," he said, "to set off tomorrow for Dunkirk with the other convicts. It is only twelve miles from this place and the party will be under my command until we reach that city. And I will permit you to travel in a wagon in order that you may have as comfortable a journey as possible."

We gratefully accepted his proposal and the next morning, just as he had promised, he sent a wagon which conveyed us to Dunkirk. Thus we rode while the other prisoners, thirty in number, were chained together and compelled to make the journey on foot. In the evening after the day's march, the head Constable invited us to supper and we were provided with a comfortable lodging for the night, so that the people of Ypres, Furnes, and other towns through which we passed, imagined us to be persons of high rank. But alas, all this consideration was like the smoke which soon vanishes away.

On the third day after our departure from Lisle, we arrived at Dunkirk and were divided with the other prisoners among the different Galleys stationed there at that time. A common sized Galley is about one hundred and fifty feet long and forty feet wide. It has fifty benches of oars, with twenty-five on each side. These benches are ten feet long and are placed at a distance of four feet from each other. On each bench sit five rowers and their work, particularly if they are made to row for long periods at a time, is exceedingly difficult and fatiguing.

The Galley to which we were sent, that is, previous to our being assigned to our particular masters, was fastened[1] to another which bore the name of the Palm-Tree, and the master of this Galley was more like a demon in his conduct than a creature that could be called human. In general, the Galleys were cleaned only once per week, but he chose to have his cleaned every day, while he stood by loading the unhappy slaves with the most terrible menaces and often striking them fearfully. My fellow-rowers often said to me, "Pray God that, in the division about to take place, you may not be appointed to the Palm-Tree."

When the day came, we drew lots for the places we were to occupy and the master to whom my lot assigned

---

1. Attached, that is, in service.

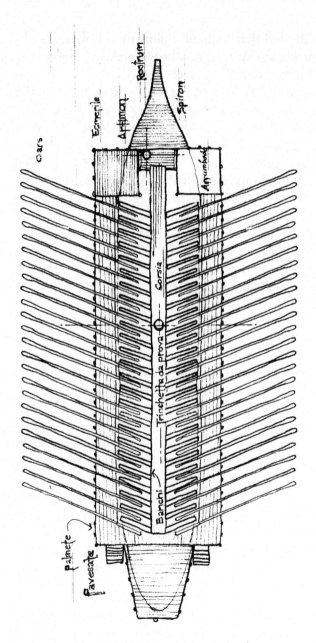

A 17th Century Galley.

me desired that I should follow him. I obeyed and, not knowing at that time that he was to be my future master, I ventured to ask to which Galley I was appointed. He answered, "To the Palm-Tree." Upon hearing this, I broke out into loud lamentations to which, he who was my conductor to that vessel asked, "Why do you think yourself more unfortunate than your companions?" "Ah, sir!" I replied, "Because I am condemned to a Galley which is said to resemble the place of torment itself and the master of which is said to be more wicked than the devil." Little did I know to whom I was addressing my complaints. He looked at me with a stern and gloomy expression of countenance. "If," he said, "I knew who had told you this and I had them in my power, I would soon make them repent of it."

The jailer from the prison had fastened around my waist an iron ring to which was attached an unusually heavy chain. He had done so, thinking that it was necessary to secure me fast on account of my youth and activity. My master, perhaps in order to prove to me that he was not as cruel as he had been represented to me, had my chain exchanged for a lighter one, which he chose himself. Indeed, I have to thank him for many indulgences during the period that I remained under his command. It is true that he exercised some severity in performing the duties of his office, but when not engaged in his business, his conduct was respectable and his manners courteous. There were five Protestants in his Galley, who never experienced ill treatment at his hands. On the contrary, he took every opportunity of showing them kindness.

An expedition against English and Dutch ships was undertaken every year by these six Galleys, which were manned by a total of three hundred men. The prisoners,

A 17th Century Galley – *side view cutaway.*

who were continually employed at the oars, were often on these occasions in great peril of their lives.[1] I shall only mention one instance that occurred in 1707. One fine morning when we were in the harbor at Dunkirk, the Commander of the Galleys, M. de Langeron, assembled the pilots of the different vessels to consult together on the state of the weather. "Was there any reason to expect a change?" he asked. To which they declared with one voice that the east wind promised a continuance of such a fine season. We were obliged to be sure of a calm sea before we ventured out, because the Galleys were not constructed in such a manner that enabled them to weather a storm.

The pilot of our Galley, however, had not expressed his opinion. His name was Peter Bart and he was a fisherman from Dunkirk and well acquainted with the coast. He was also the natural brother of the celebrated northern Admiral John Bart, but he was a notorious drunkard. Nevertheless, he was a very experienced seaman and an attentive observer of the changes in the weather. He was, however, in little credit with his fellow steersmen[2] on account of his drunken habits. He was generally in a state of intoxication and his language was coarse and familiar.[3] The Commander, turning to him, asked what he thought of the weather. "Will you go to sea?" he said. "I promise you," replied Bart, "it will be boiled enough by tomorrow morning." But they only

---

1. "Chained to a bench of his Galley, the poor prisoner remained there night and day, with felons for his companions, and scarcely any clothing, scorched by the sun, frozen by the cold, or drenched by the sea, and compelled to row at the utmost of his strength—and if, being exhausted, he let the oar drop, he was sure to be visited with the bastinado. Such was the sufferings amid which hundreds of Protestants of France wore out long years." *La Société de l'Histoire du Protestantisme Français* (1853).

2. The person who steers a ship; the helmsman.

3. Unceremonious.

laughed at him and although he earnestly begged to be left on shore the Commander would not grant his request. Our Galleys, together with those under the command of M. de Fontete, put to sea. The water was so unruffled and the day was so calm that a lighted candle might have been placed on the mast head without blowing out.

At sea the next morning, we came to the roads[1] of Ambleteuse, a little village lying between Calais and Boulogne. Beyond the roads was a bay sheltered from the east and north-east winds by a mountain on each side of it. I do not know what induced our Commander to anchor in the bay. M. de Fontete was much more prudent and remained in the roads. When Peter Bart saw us prepare to cast anchor he called out in a tone of despair, saying that we must not run the Galley into the bay. On our asking the reason for this, he added that at daybreak the next morning a terrible storm would arise from the south-west and that we would not then be able to leave the bay. The entrance to the bay being open exactly into the wind from that quarter,[2] so that our Galleys would be driven upon the rocks and be so split to pieces that all on board must surely perish.

His words, however, were disregarded and the anchors being cast a little before day, we lay down to obtain a short interval of repose. Peter Bart continued to groan and weep like one who expected inevitable death. At length daylight appeared. The wind blew from the south-west, but so gently that no notice was taken of it. But scarcely had the morning rays gilded the horizon when the increased violence of the wind drew the

---

1. The 'roads' is a place where ships may rest safe at anchor at a distance from the shore; it is a place for 'riding' at anchor.
2. Direction.

attention of the most incredulous[1] to the warnings of the pilot which he had often repeated. We received orders to leave the bay, but before we could accomplish our purpose the tempest raged with such fury that instead of weighing anchor,[2] we were obliged to throw out two more anchors in order to stand against the violence of the winds and waves. This we did while every moment the foaming deep discovered[3] to us new rocks, which threatened our vessels with destruction. And what made the danger more imminent was that the anchors we had cast from the fore part of the Galley would not fix,[4] and so we were driven against the rocks. We attempted to row toward the anchors, but at the moment we let down our oars, they were carried away by the violence of the waves. The alarm now became so general that nothing was to be heard but loud lamentations and cries for deliverance. The priest on board administered the holy sacrament and gave absolution to those who declared themselves truly penitent for their past sins, there being neither time nor opportunity for their confessions. The slaves who were condemned for their crimes to labor at the oars, far from showing any signs of contrition, called out loudly to their Commander and Officers, "A little patience, gentlemen! We shall soon be together as equals and drink from the same glass." So true is it that the impenitent heart will not always be softened even by the sight of approaching death.

In this emergency, when destruction seemed inevitable, our Commander noticed Peter Bart, who was standing apart from the rest and looked very downcast. "Ah, Peter!" he said to him, "Had I believed you, we would

---

1. Unbelieving.
2. Raising the anchor.
3. Revealed.
4. Did not hold the Galley.

not now be in danger. But do you know any means whereby we may escape?" "What use is there," answered Peter, "in my giving you advice, since you do not listen to a word I say. Yes, I do know a way by which, with God's assistance, we may be saved from shipwreck. But I tell you fairly[1] that were it not that I love my own life too well you might drown like so many pigs for all the help I would give you." His rudeness passed unnoticed since he had kindled a ray of hope in every heart. And Peter went on: "I further declare that if I undertake the business to save our lives, I will not allow any opposition in any of my arrangements, although they may at first sight appear useless and even ridiculous. My orders must be obeyed or we shall all perish."

The Commander instantly desired that implicit obedience should be paid to Peter's orders—under pain of death. The pilot then demanded the Commander's purse. "Here it is," said the Commander, "do what you please with it." When Peter had taken four louis d'ors out of the purse, he returned it to its owner and then asked whether there were four men present who would undertake a dangerous service, promising the reward of a louis d'or to each if they succeeded. Twenty men instantly came forward of whom, however, he selected only four who were noted for their courage. These he placed in the boat belonging to the Galley and, giving them an anchor, the rope of which was fastened to the vessel, he desired them to cast it at the hinder part.[2] We all wondered at this plan, for we could not imagine of what use the anchor would be at the hinder part of the Galley, since it was the fore part we wished to be secured. The Commander himself was anxious to know

---

1. Honestly.
2. Cast anchor from the stern of the ship.

what this anchor was expected to effect, but Peter only answered him saying, "You will see in time enough, if it pleases God." After great pains and much risk, the mariners were at length successful in their enterprise and fixed the anchor on the rock. When Peter saw this accomplished, he seized the Commander's hand exclaiming, "Praised be God, we are safe!" However, none of us could guess what plan he had in mind.

Peter now lowered the yard,[1] fastened the sail-cloth to it, rolled it up and wound it round with reeds which, when the ropes were cut, would of course break and leave the sail to spread itself at liberty. He then had the sail raised again and desired that four sailors be ready to cut the cables the moment he gave the word of command. The rope attached to the anchor at the stern of the vessel was tightened and a sailor was stationed with an axe to cut it when the order was given. After all these preparations, he commanded the men at the fore part of the Galley to cut the ropes of the anchors. As soon as this part of the Galley was free, it turned around. Peter's skill allowed it, only to turn as far as necessary in order to get wind for the sail. As soon as the sail was raised, the reeds were torn in pieces and the sail spread itself and filled with wind. At the same time, the anchor at the stern was cut loose and Peter seized the helm and ran the Galley with the utmost rapidity out of the unlucky bay. His skill had thus rescued us from imminent danger and we found ourselves once more on the open sea.

We now sailed for Dunkirk and soon entered the roads. Here we cast two anchors lent to us by M. de Fontete. We were obliged to wait six hours for the tide, during

---

1. The timber that is suspended on the mast and from which the sail is extended.

which interval we appeared to be hovering between life and death. The mountain high waves rolled over the vessel and covered us with spray. And had not the doors and other openings of the deck been carefully secured, the hold would have been under water and the Galley would have sunk. The inhabitants of the city, who saw our danger from the shore, joined in prayer for our deliverance and public masses were offered for us in all the churches of Dunkirk. This was the only assistance they could offer us in our desperate condition. At length, the returning tide permitted us to make a final effort for our preservation by endeavoring to enter the harbor. But this attempt was also accompanied by great danger, because the vessel must necessarily turn short round between two points of the dyke which enclose the harbor and the length of the ship would render this particularly difficult. And besides all this, the front of the dyke was so swollen by the violence of the sea that it was only at intervals, when the waves divided for a moment, that we could clearly distinguish the entrance. What was to be done?

We called Peter Bart, who was quietly asleep on a bench, not regarding the waves, which rolled continually over his head. The Commander asked him whether he thought it possible to enter the harbor. "Certainly," he replied, "I will take you in with full sails." "What!" returned the Commander, "With, full sails? Then we will all be lost." "Fear nothing," said Peter, "all will yet be well." We were by this time more dead than alive, shivering with the cold and wet, for we were up to our knees in water. And we were almost famished with hunger because we had not tasted food for nearly three days, not venturing to open the door of the store-room lest we should let in the water and sink the vessel. And now we were in expectation of being dashed in pieces against the entrance of the dyke. But Peter laughed at what he called womanish fears, adding, however, that he could not ensure that the prow would not be broken, for the wind was so strong that it would not be possible to prevent the Galley from running against the fish market, which adjoined the harbor. The cables were cut and our pilot guided the helm with such skill that he turned round into the entrance of the dyke without injury to the vessel. And then, spreading the sail, the Galley ran, as he had foretold, against the fish market with such speed that two or three hundred sailors, who had been sent to our assistance and who stood upon the dyke, could not hold us in with their ropes, which broke like thread from the violence of the wind.

This disastrous voyage thus happily over. Our Commander very much wished to retain Peter Bart in his vessel, promising him double wages if he would continue in his service. But nothing could induce the pilot to remain. "I would be a fool to stay with you," he said, "though you were to pay me a thousand livres a month." And with that he took his leave.

On another occasion in September, 1708, our vessels engaged in combat with an English Frigate.[1] I received three wounds, which for three days were without surgical care. In this miserable condition, I was returned to Dunkirk where I was conveyed to the hospital with the rest of the wounded. In the Dunkirk hospital the slaves were separated from the other mariners and placed in two large rooms that each contained forty beds. About one o'clock in the afternoon, the head naval surgeon, accompanied by all the surgeons belonging to the ships and Galleys which were at that time in the harbor, came to dress our wounds. I had

---

1. A smaller warship that began to be used in the late 1600's.

In combat with an English
Frigate in 1708.

"The two vessels lay so close, by raising my body in
the least, I could touch the cannon with my hand.
Since I was chained, it was impossible to leave
my station. In this manner then, I awaited death."
*Condemned to the Galleys: The Adventures of a French
Protestant*, the memoirs of Jean Martielhe.

been specifically recommended to his care—and how this happened, I must go back a little in my history to explain.

Ever since my arrival in the Galleys in the year 1702, I had been recommended by the efforts of my relations to the protection of Mr. Piecourt, who was a rich banker who had a house at Dunkirk, where he also lived during the greater part of the year. Mr. Piecourt had received letters on the subject of my welfare from Bordeaux, Bergerac, and Amsterdam. Being himself a native of Bergerac and at heart a Protestant—although he externally conformed to the rites of the Romish Church—and further, having received letters in my favor from persons whose friendship he valued, he thought it worthwhile to take some trouble to show me kindness and indeed, if possible to procure my freedom. He spoke in my behalf to M. de Langeron, with whom he was particularly acquainted, and by his intercession I was allowed many indulgences. Wishing still further to serve me, one day he obtained permission from M. de Langeron to take me home with him on the following morning. It was on Christmas day, not long after my arrival at Dunkirk, and it was during the hour of Divine service, while his wife was at church, that with the consent of our Commander I accompanied Mr. Piecourt to his house. He took me into his study and, having first assured me of how anxious he was to show me all the kindness that was in his power, he explained that he had contrived a means of procuring my freedom—if I would consent to his plan.

I thanked him for his kindness, and said I would willingly do what he desired if it does not go against my conscience. "Conscience," he returned, "must indeed have a share in the business, but so small a share that you need feel no compunction,[1] and even if you disapprove the proceeding, you may give it up when you get to Holland."

"Now observe," he continued, "that I am a Protestant like yourself, but my circumstances demand that I must represent myself to be a Catholic. Nor can I believe this to be a sin as I do not in heart turn away from the true faith. Now then, this also is to be the means whereby I hope to establish and maintain your liberty. M. de Ponchartrain, the Minister of Marine, is my friend and will not refuse any request I make to him. If you will agree, you must subscribe[2] a paper containing a promise that if you are set at liberty you will live and die a good Catholic, even if you eventually settle out of France. On my part then, I will ensure that, without being compelled to make a public abjuration of your Protestant faith or being made to take any steps that might excite the suspicion of your brethren, you shall be set free before a fortnight has elapsed. And further, I pledge myself to get you to Holland without your incurring the smallest danger."

"Sir," I replied, "I have been greatly deceived in supposing you to be a Protestant, nor can I express the indignation I feel at your proposal. You must pardon me if I say that, whatever you may call yourself, you are not worthy of the name of Protestant. What, sir! Do you suppose the Almighty to be unmindful of your conduct? And do you not feel that the promise that you make me, and which is to be concealed from men, even if it could it be annulled by an earthly judge, would

---

1. Remorse or regret for having done something that is sinful and offensive to God.

2. To bind oneself by a written contract or promise by affirming the thing written with one's own signature.

only so much the more offend against God's Divine Majesty? Sir, do not be deceived. Your own conscience must condemn you, for you know assuredly that if our outward behavior does not agree with the conviction of our hearts, this conviction will only add to our sin."

Mr. Piecourt tried to overcome my scruples, alleging that the Gospel did not require so much strictness. But I resisted his arguments as contrary to my conscience, adding that those who had recommended me to his favor would by no means wish me to purchase my freedom by any departure from the Protestant faith. "No, indeed," he answered, "nor can I wish to press you any further on the subject." He then embraced me with tearful eyes and prayed God to preserve me in a determination so worthy of a professor of the true religion of Christ. "From henceforth," he continued, "I shall love you not only on account of the many letters of recommendation I have received on your behalf, but also from my own observation of your worth. And you may be well assured that I shall take every opportunity of serving you."

From this time Mr. Piecourt often visited me at the Galleys and on all occasions showed me uniform kindness. On the 17th of September, 1708, as soon as he had heard that our Galley had been engaged with the English Frigate and had lost many of her crew, he ran directly down to the harbor to make inquiries after me. It was upon being told that I had been wounded and had already been taken to the hospital, that he immediately went to the head surgeon with whom he was acquainted, and commended me as earnestly to his attention as if I had been his own son.

I must add that, under God, I owe to this surgeon the preservation of my life and I will always feel the most sincere gratitude towards him. A third part of the men who were wounded died in the hospital and of these, many were not nearly as severely hurt as myself. In less than two months my wounds were cured, but I remained another month in the hospital to recruit my strength. They took as much care of me as if I had been a prince and in three months, I was as strong and as fat as a monk. But on account of the lameness which had settled in my arm, I was removed from the oars, where I had labored for seven years, and appointed to the store room. Soon afterwards, I obtained the office of clerk to the Commander and my situation became wonderfully improved. Indeed, I now lacked nothing but freedom. I was no longer encumbered by a chain, either day or night, and was made to wear only a ring around my foot. I was allowed to sleep in a comfortable bed, while the rest of my companions labored at the oars. Thus I remained until the year 1712.

CHAPTER 7
THE JOURNEY TO MARSEILLES

CHAPTER 7
THE JOURNEY TO MARSEILLES

 t was in the year 1712, when the court of France, having agreed to give up to the English government the city of Dunkirk with its fortifications and its harbor, that the slaves in the Galleys which were stationed there at that time, were transferred to Marseilles. We began our journey on the 1st of October; we went by Havre de Grace to Paris. We had been at Havre for a fortnight when one evening at about nine o'clock, as we were eating our scanty meal, our guards having gone to supper also, I felt someone touch me on the shoulder. Turning around, I saw the young lady who was the daughter of the principal banker in the city. She held in her hand a volume of sermons that I had lent her a few days before. These she returned to me saying hastily, "Here is your book. May God be with you in all your troubles. Tonight at twelve o'clock you will leave this place. Four wagons are ordered to convey you away. The white gate will be left open for you to pass through. You will be taken to a prison in Paris and from there you will be sent to Marseilles. May you continue firm in all the trials of your faith."

We remained quietly eating our suppers, making no remark on what had happened. But when we had finished our meal, instead of lying down to sleep on our mattresses, we began to gather our few belongings together in readiness to set off. While we were thus employed, our overseer came in as usual to spend an hour with us, which he passed in talking and smoking his pipe. When he saw that we were packing up our things instead of preparing our beds he asked with some surprise, what we were going to do. "We are getting ready for our journey," I replied. "You are a fool," he answered. "What do you mean by such nonsense?" "I tell you," I continued, "that at twelve o'clock this very night, four wagons will be at the entrance of the arsenal. They will convey us through the white gate and we shall go to Paris, and from there we shall travel to Marseilles." "I repeat that you are a fool," answered the overseer, "and that there is not the slightest truth in what you say. I saw the Commandant at eight o'clock this evening and he gave only the usual orders." "Very well, sir," I replied, "you will soon hear."

Scarcely had we finished the conversation, when a servant belonging to the Commandant entered and told the overseer that his master wished to speak to him immediately. He returned shortly after in the greatest astonishment. "Tell me," he exclaimed, "whether you are sorcerers or prophets. I believe, however, that God is with you, for you are too honest and pious to have dealings with the devil." "No, indeed, we are neither prophets nor sorcerers. The matter is simple enough." "I do not understand it at all," returned the overseer, "for the Commandant has just assured me that no one in the city knows of our intended departure besides himself. I must, then, believe that God is especially with you." "I trust so," I replied and we all immediately prepared for our journey.

The mystery was easily explained. The daughter of the banker was engaged to be married to the secretary of the Commandant, and from him she had learned the secret. As we proceeded on the road to Paris, we were met by numbers of Protestants, who, regardless of the blows that were being liberally bestowed upon them by the rude[1] constables in order to disperse them, pressed forward to embrace us and encourage us by words of comfort. The red dress[2] worn by the prisoners who were Protestant, of whom there were twenty-two, made them easily distinguishable from the other prisoners and these worthy people, among whom were many of the higher classes, addressed us saying, "Take comfort you confessors of the truth. Suffer boldly in so noble a cause. We shall not cease to pray for you, that God would show you his mercy and support you in all your afflictions."

We passed through Charenton, the Isle of France, Burgundy, and Maçon, and to Lyons, travelling at the rate of three or four miles per day. This was a long walk for persons encumbered by heavy fetters[3] and suffering numberless privations. Our food was of the poorest kind and our only couch was a dirty stable. During the day we often walked in mud up to our knees, while a tempest was beating upon our heads and the rain drenching us to the skin. Add to this the filth and the vermin,[4] which were the necessary consequence of our misery.

---

1. Fierce.

2. The outfit furnished to the Protestant prisoners to distinguish their particular 'crime' of faith in the Protestant religion.

3. Chains upon a prisoner's feet.

4. Without bathing and fresh clothes, the prisoners would have been subject to lice and other miseries.

We embarked at Lyons and went by boat up the river Rhone until we came to the bridge "den Heiligen Geist." From there we went by land to Avignon and then on to Marseilles, where we arrived on the 7th of January, 1713.

The prisoners who were Protestants were all in perfect health, but many of the other prisoners had died on the road. Most of them had become ill and not a few expired in the hospital at Marseilles soon after our arrival. Thus we completed our journey from Dunkirk to Marseilles. During this journey, especially after we left Paris, I suffered more than I had done during the twelve previous years of my captivity and labor at the oars.

At Marseilles we were placed in the principal Galley. Here we found many fellow-sufferers for the Protestant faith. The Protestants in the vessel at this time were forty in number. Our brethren received us with open arms and hailed our arrival with mingled emotions of pain and pleasure—pleasure to see us in good health and steadfast in the will of the Most High, and pain on account of the trials we had endured. And here we united in praise to Him who had enabled us to withstand such long and dangerous temptations.

CHAPTER 8
DELIVERANCE

CHAPTER 8
DELIVERANCE

 fter the Peace of Ryswick,[1] the Popish priests were very anxious that the Protestant slaves should be compelled to uncover their heads and prostrate themselves[2] on the earth in the same manner as the Catholics did during the celebration of mass. And by the persuasions of these missionaries, M. de Bonbelle was induced to inflict the punishment of the lash on all who refused to comply with this order. M. de Bonbelle went daily from vessel to vessel to see that this decree was enforced He admonished the sufferers to obedience with such blasphemous expressions as these: "Down, dog, on your knees when mass is read, and in this position worship either God or the devil—it is the same to us." Of those, upon whom this punishment was inflicted, not one yielded to the temptation of escaping the lash by worshipping on the ground. All remained firm and praised God amidst their sufferings. The ambassadors of the Protestant powers, being informed of these atrocities, however, made such strong representations to the King on the subject that orders were soon afterwards sent forbidding personal

---

1. Signed in 1697, the treaty ended the Nine Years' War between France, Spain, England, the United Provinces (the Dutch Republic), and the Holy Roman Empire.

2. In worship of the eucharistic elements which are believed by them to have become the real body and blood of Jesus Christ.

violence to be used to enforce the submission of the Protestant slaves.

When the Peace of Utrecht[1] was concluded without any stipulation in our behalf, the Marquis de Rochegude, a French nobleman who had taken refuge in Switzerland,

Queen Anne of England, who was instrumental in securing the release of the Huguenot Galley slaves of France.

determined to make a last effort to succor his persecuted countrymen. He went from Utrecht into Sweden to King Charles XII, and from there he went to the Kings of Denmark and Prussia. In short, he traveled to all the Protestant Princes in Europe and obtained from each of them letters of introduction to Anne, the Queen of England, in which they entreated her to interpose for our deliverance. He then

---

1. The Peace of Utrecht ended the War of the Spanish Succession and although the Huguenots, many of whom had previously fled France and were resident in foreign lands, had persuaded the Protestant rulers of England, Holland, and Prussia to place the question of the civil and religious rights of the French Huguenots on the agenda in consideration of the upcoming peace, none of these powers was prepared to make the fate of the Huguenots a real condition of that peace. Thus, the issue of the French King's policy of imprisoning his Protestant subjects was taken up immediately—*and effectively*—afterward by the Protestant powers of Europe.

delivered these letters to the Queen and when, after a fortnight had elapsed, he requested her answer, she said to him, "I pray you, M. de Rochegude, send word to the poor Galley slaves that they shall soon be set at liberty."[1] The Marquis lost no time in conveying this welcome intelligence to us through the Geneva post.

In some degree it revived our hopes, although we had long ceased to expect human help. And indeed, we thanked God for this fresh proof of his mercy. A short time afterwards, the Commandant at Marseilles received orders from the government to send a list of the Protestant prisoners who were held at that time in Marseilles. This he did and at the end of May, he received another communication from the court, desiring that he set at liberty a certain number of Protestants. The rest—for there were about three hundred of us—were not dismissed until the following year.

The Commandant, having informed the Popish missionaries that orders had been given to dismiss the Protestant slaves, declared with indignation that the King must have been grossly deceived, and that it would be an eternal disgrace to the Romish Church if the heretics were to be set at liberty. They requested the Commandant, therefore, delay the execution of the decree for a fortnight, during which time they proposed sending an express courier to the court in order, if possible, to persuade the government to countermand the King's order. Their request was granted and the King's letter was kept a profound secret. Nevertheless, a

---

1. Queen Anne demanded the liberation of the Huguenot slaves from the French Galleys and, after much vacillation on the part of King Louis XIV, a number of the Huguenots were released. More effort was expended by this Queen in order to secure the liberation of the remaining Huguenot Galley slaves, *as will be seen as our history progresses.*

report to the effect that some of the Protestants were to be freed from their long captivity reached our ears, and we even learned, a little at a time, the names of those who were mentioned in the list. My name was the last in the catalogue, and for three days I remained in uncertainty whether I was put down on the list at all.

At last, I was relieved from this anxiety, although we were all in much apprehension regarding our fate when we heard of the proceedings of the Popish priests. The courier returned to Marseilles, bringing no answer, good or bad, from the court. Upon this, however, the missionaries obtained another week's delay, hoping that another express courier, which they had dispatched immediately after the first, might bring an answer more favorable to their designs. But the second messenger also returned without any communication from the government. The Popish priests no longer had any pretext for opposing our freedom. But, by their malicious suggestions, the Commandant was induced to impose this condition, namely, that we should immediately embark on board some vessel and leave the kingdom at our own expense. It was difficult for us to promise obedience, as there was no ship in the harbor that was about to sail for Holland or England, and we could not afford to hire a ship for ourselves.

At last, a pilot of one of the Galleys, Jovas by name, told one of our brethren that he would take us from Marseilles to Villefranche, a seaport in the county of Nice, which belonged to the King of Sardinia, and from there we might go through Piedmont to Geneva.[1] He

---

1. Geneva was a safe haven for the Protestants, and the mountains and valleys of the Piedmont had been a haven for the Gospel believing peoples of the middle ages, who were commonly known as Waldenses or Vaudois.

had a Tartane[1] of his own, that is, one of those boats called by that name that were usually employed upon the Mediterranean. We agreed to give this man six livres each for our passage, out of which he was to supply us with provisions.[2] This was a liberal payment for a short voyage of twenty-five miles. Thus, notwithstanding the opposition of the priests, we left Marseilles on the 17th of June, 1713.

Although we had a favorable wind, the sea was very rough and the boat was so tossed by the waves that we expected at any moment to be overturned. Every person suffered terribly from sea-sickness. Jovas landed the Tartane at Villefranche and said he had business in Nice, where he also wished to attend mass. I asked permission to accompany him into the town, to which he willingly consented. Thus we set out together with some of my brethren joining us. At the entrance of the town, our Captain said he would go to mass, and told us that we had better wait for him at the nearest inn. We turned into one of the principal streets and, it being Sunday and all the shops and houses were shut, we met scarcely any one at all on the street.

We had not gone far, however, before we saw a man coming towards us. At first, we hardly noticed him, but as he approached us and greeted us with great civility, he said that he hoped that we would not be displeased if he took the liberty of inquiring where we had come from. We told him that we had come from Marseilles. He hesitated a moment, desiring to ask but not liking to ask us directly whether we were from the Galleys— it being considered a great affront to say that a man

---

1. Or 'Tartan;' a small coasting vessel with a single mast and bowsprit, and a very large triangular shaped sail.

2. Food and necessities.

has been put to work on the Galleys unless, indeed, he has been captive there on account of his religion. Thus phrasing his inquiry with the greatest care, "I pray you, Gentlemen," he continued, "tell me whether you left Marseilles by order of the King." "Yes, sir," we replied, "we have come from the French Galleys." "God be praised," he exclaimed, "you are among the number of those persons who are only lately dismissed on account of their religion?" And upon our answering in the affirmative, the man was almost beside himself with joy and requested of us that we would follow him to his house. This we did without much thought or consideration, although Jovas, who remained with us, was not without some anxiety as to what the result might be, knowing, as he did, that it was not always very safe to trust the Italians.

The stranger conducted us to his mansion, which appeared to us to be more like the palace of a nobleman than the dwelling of a merchant. As we entered his home, he embraced us with tears of joy and then he called for his wife and children. "Come," he cried, "and welcome our brethren, who at last have been delivered from their heavy afflictions in the Galleys." After which Signor Bonijoli, for this was the merchant's name, begged us to unite with him in prayer. We knelt down together and Signor Bonijoli offered up a fervent thanksgiving for our deliverance. We all wept, and Jovas, who knelt down with us, assured us afterwards that he felt as if he were transported to paradise. When the prayer was concluded, breakfast was brought to us and we continued over breakfast to have much pious conversation about the mighty power of God, who had granted us grace to abide firm in the faith and to be more than conquerors over our enemies.

Afterward, Signor Bonijoli asked us how many we were in number. We told him, "Thirty-six." "This agrees with my letter," he answered, "for I must tell you that one of my correspondents at Marseilles told me what day you were to be discharged from the Galleys and had requested of me that I locate you and show you any kindness that was in my power if you should pass through Nice. But where are the rest?" "At Villefranche," we replied. Signor Bonijoli immediately sent to invite them to Nice. Upon their arrival, he received them with the greatest hospitality and arranged for their boarding at the best hotels, desiring that they should be entertained in the most liberal manner at his own expense. We, who had first made his acquaintance, remained in his house and during our month long residence in Nice, we had to thank him for daily proofs of his friendship. Jovas, at the end of this period, returned to Marseilles, promising that he would advise our brethren, who were to follow in two other vessels, to go also by way of Villefranche.

After the departure of Jovas, Signer Bonijoli hastened to make arrangements for our journey northward and, at his own expense, hired thirty-six mules and a guide to take us as far as Turin. At last we left Nice at the beginning of July. We had several very aged persons in our party, which rather slowed our progress because they could scarcely sit upright on their mules by reason of their infirmities. Our road led us over mountains, amongst which was the Col di Tenda. Although at the foot of this mountain we suffered from the extreme heat, yet when we reached the summit, the cold was so intense that we were obliged to alight from our mules and walk in order to keep ourselves warm. We descended on the other side of the mountains into the plain of Piedmont, a rich and beautiful country, and soon we arrived at Turin in safety.

A view of Turin.

Signor Bonijoli had written letters of introduction on our behalf to the Protestants of Turin. Many of these people were engaged in different trades in Turin, but all professed the same faith as the inhabitants of the Waldensian valleys. The Protestants of Turin received us with brotherly affection and entertained us for three days, after which they requested the King to give us a passport that would enable us to travel in security through his dominions to Geneva; these kind people having provided beasts for us to continue our journey there.

Before our departure, King Victor Amadeus having expressed a wish to see us, six of us were brought and presented to him. This audience occurred in the presence of the English and Dutch Ambassadors. The King received us very graciously and conversed with us for half an hour, during which he asked us various questions including, "How long we had been at the Galleys? Why we had left them?" and "How we were employed there?" And when we had answered all of his questions, he addressed the Ambassadors saying, "This is cruel and barbarous."

His Majesty then asked us whether we had sufficient money for our journey to Geneva. To this, we replied that we had not much money, but that Signor Bonijoli had sent us free of expense from Nice to Turin and that our Protestant brethren in Turin were providing the same for us as far as Geneva. Upon hearing this, his Majesty went on to tell us that we might remain in Turin as long as we liked and when we wished to leave Turin, we needed only to speak to his secretary who would immediately give us a passport.[1] In this passport, all the subjects of King Victor Amadeus were commanded to receive us and to provide us with all things necessary for our journey. Praised be to God, though, we were never obliged to make use of it as our brethren at Turin, who had already loaded us with favors, also sent us on at their own expense to Geneva.

At the time we were in Turin, we became acquainted with a young man that was a watchmaker by trade, who was a native of Geneva. Upon setting off to Geneva, he accompanied us on foot during the greater part of

---

1. Remembering that a passport in the early eighteenth century was not the same as that issued in modern times; it may have been issued for the whole party and was a specific license from a king or authorized authority that granted a safe conduct for passage through a specific territory, that is, permission to travel or pass through a place without hindrance by any persons living there.

our journey. When we were about two days' distance from Geneva he took leave of us saying that he knew a footpath across the country, which was much nearer than the high road and that would bring him to the town a day sooner than we ourselves would arrive. Accordingly, he arrived there the day before us and told his acquaintance that thirty-six French Protestants, who had just lately been discharged from the Galleys, were on their way there. This introduction, having reached the ears of the Chief Magistrate, he immediately sent a messenger to make inquiries respecting us.

The next morning, our road led us over a mountain, about one mile south of Geneva. From the top of the mountain, when we saw the city directly in front of us, our emotions must have resembled those feelings which the Israelites must have experienced at the first sight of the land of Canaan after so long a journey in the wilderness. As we arrived on a Sunday, the gates of the city were not yet open and would only be opened after Divine Service, that is, after about four o'clock in the afternoon. We were, therefore, obliged to wait some hours in the neighboring village. Scarcely had our little party set out from there on our final march into Geneva, when we perceived a crowd of persons advancing towards us from that town. Our guide appeared much astonished and he was still more astonished when, having arrived upon the plain about a quarter of an hour's walk from the city, we were met by three coaches escorted by halberdiers[1] and followed by a throng of people. The crowd opened as we approached and a

---

1. Soldiers armed with halberds. A halberd, also known as a pole ax, consisted of a long shaft of wood tipped with a broad flat blade that was a sharp ax on one side, had a hook, known as a 'beak,' on the other, and terminated in a spear point. The hook was used to pull a rider off his horse and to pierce armor. The Swiss were particularly known for their skill in the use of this weapon.

Geneva – in about the year 1700.

servant of the local Prefect,[1] respectfully accosting[2] us, announced that his master was come in person to congratulate us on our arrival at Geneva. As he spoke, several magistrates and clergymen alighted from the coaches and embraced us with the warmest affection. These also congratulated us on our constancy in the faith of Jesus Christ. And this they did in a manner that seemed far beyond our poor deserts. We thanked them with deep emotion and magnified the grace of God which had helped us through so many difficulties. In their turn, the people now began to salute us with much kindness. But what a scene followed! Many inhabitants of Geneva had relations or friends in the Galleys and, as they were ignorant as to whether some of them were among us or not, cries were heard on all sides: "My husband, my son, my brother are you there?" We were almost suffocated with embraces, and it was not without difficulty that we persuaded them to allow us to remount our mules and enter the town. There we were conducted in triumph, and the inhabitants of the city contended with each other for the pleasure of receiving us into their homes.

I and six others of my brethren remained only a very short time at Geneva. We hired a coach which, in fact, had just brought the Prussian Ambassador from Berlin to Geneva, which coach we desired to take us as far as Frankfort, from which we hoped to continue our journey to Holland. The gentlemen at Geneva had the goodness to pay our travelling expenses and to present us with an extra sum of money besides. En route to Frankfort, we stayed four days in Berne, where we were treated with the same respect and liberality. Upon our

---

1. The Chief Magistrate.
2. Approaching face to face in order to speak first.

departure from that place, the Burgomaster[1] gave us twenty dollars for our journey.

A view of Berne.

At the beginning of August, we reached Frankfort. The gentlemen at Geneva had commended us to the attention of M. Sarasin, a merchant in that city who was also a member of the Reformed church at Bochenheim, which was near Frankfort. At that time there was no place of worship for the Protestants at Frankfort, so that they were obliged to attend Divine Service at Bochenheim. We went to M. Sarasin's house, and in a short time all the members of the congregation were assembled. Among the congregation were many French and German people, who received us with great

---

1. The Chief Magistrate of the town or 'burg.'

pleasure and took us with them to Bochenheim. At the church there we heard a sermon preached by M. Matthieu, the French pastor.

Afterward, M. Sarasin most kindly made the necessary arrangements for us to continue our journey. He purchased a small vessel to take us to Cologne, furnished us with provisions for our journey, and desired of the sailors that they touch land at different places along the way in order that we might have the comfort of passing the night on shore. He also particularly warned the crew of the ship to keep as near as possible to that side of the river along which the Imperial Army was at that time encamped, because otherwise we would incur the danger of being apprehended by the French, who were on the other side of the river and engaged in the Siege of Landau. Before we embarked, M. Sarasin accompanied us to the Council House, to procure passports. The magistrates who were present wished us much happiness—calling us "the salt of the earth," but far from being flattered by their commendations, we felt deeply humbled on account of our unworthiness to receive them, and we gave God the glory. I saw several of the gentlemen weeping in sympathy for our past sufferings, while they admonished us to continue steadfast in the Protestant faith. Passports were given us, for which we were not allowed to pay, and we took leave of both the magistrates and M. Sarasin with the deepest feelings of gratitude.

Our voyage to Holland was somewhat tedious, because the sentinels of the Imperial Army that were stationed on the bank of the river were continually detaining us to examine our passports. Although the French discharged several shots at us from the other side, yet, praise be to God, we escaped without injury. A week after our departure from Frankfort, we arrived at Cologne. In Cologne we sold our vessel and continued on in the public boat to Dort. From Dort we proceeded immediately through Rotterdam and on to Amsterdam.

I have only time to mention, very briefly, the affectionate reception we met with from our Protestant brethren in that city. We were introduced into the consistory of the church where we rendered our sincere thanks to the members of the church for the assistance they afforded us during our imprisonment in the Galleys. To this they returned the answer that their assistance would be continued as long as we needed it. We were affectionately exhorted to live up to our privileges as confessors of a holy faith and that we might adorn our Christian profession by a blameless walk and conversation.

In Amsterdam we received numerous proofs of friendship toward us from every side. After we had remained three or four weeks in that city, the consistory requested that I be one of the deputies who were about to proceed to England in the name of the church, in order to return thanks to Queen Anne for the share she had taken in obtaining our deliverance, and to entreat her to exert herself still further to procure the discharge of the rest of our fellow-sufferers in the Galleys.

I went with two of our brethren to London and in a short time, the number of deputies increased to twelve, all of whom, like ourselves, were only recently dismissed from slavery. The Marquises de Miremont and de Rochegude presented us to the Queen, who graciously permitted us to kiss her hand. The Marquis de Miremont returned thanks to her Majesty in our name, to which she replied that she rejoiced to see us at liberty and that she hoped to be able to procure the

London - *in the year 1700.*

pardon of those Protestants who were still laboring in the Galleys.

By request of the Marquis de Rochegude, we were also received by the French Ambassador, M. de Aumont. The Ambassador admitted us with politeness and congratulated us on our freedom, asking how long we had served in the Galleys. In turn, we requested of him that he would petition the French government to release the rest of the Protestant slaves, adding that the King had consented to grant a free pardon to all, and yet only one hundred and thirty-six had been dismissed, while more than two hundred still remained in chains. The Ambassador appeared much surprised at this, and said that he thought they must be detained on other grounds. But we assured him that this was not the case and in proof of it I related to him how my companion, Daniel le Gras, was sentenced at the same time as myself and for a similar crime, and yet he was still a prisoner at Marseilles while I was set at liberty. This appeared to convince him and he promised to write on the subject to the French government. However, it turned out that he was persuaded by his secretary, the Abbé Nadal, to relinquish his intention of writing on behalf of the remaining Protestant prisoners. A year elapsed before our brethren were discharged and then they were discharged only in compliance with the repeated solicitations of the English Queen.

I hasten now to the conclusion of my history. With the consent of the Marquis de Rochegude, I left London after I had resided in that metropolis for about ten weeks. Several of my brethren remained behind in order to assist as far as they possibly could in the exertions of the English Queen on behalf of our friends.

Afterward, I remained some weeks at the Hague.[1] The pastor, Basnage, succeeded in obtaining a pension for us from the States-General. We had not, in the smallest degree, deserved these favors and could only ascribe them to the Christian kindness of those who showed us so much care. When I reflect upon the conduct of these gentlemen, I cannot sufficiently admire their devotion to God, their zeal for his glory, and their love to their fellow Protestants. Well did they observe the sacred precept, "Do good unto all men, especially unto them who are of the household of faith," Galatians 6:10.

> May God be the rewarder of all those benefits which were conferred upon us during this painful and weary part of our earthly pilgrimage.

Jean Martielhe

---

1. The Hague is now the provincial capital of South Holland.

It was not until 1775, at the beginning of the reign of King Louis XVI, that the Royal French Galleys released their last two Protestant prisoners.

CHAPTER 9
CONCLUDING REMARKS

CHAPTER 9
CONCLUDING REMARKS

n closing this interesting narrative, will it not be immediately felt by every reader how great our outward advantages are, who have far lighter inconveniences to suffer for the sake of religion? In the era wherein this history occurred, there were those who believed it to be agreeable to the service of God not to tolerate those who held the truth of the Gospel. They held that freedom of conscience was a mere licensable privilege, to be granted or denied at will, but persecution and force were their God given right and even their glory, the very proof of the reward they anticipated from the Almighty. Those merciless persecutors took no heed to God's Word and their rage remained unchecked.

"They shall put you out of the synagogues *(the assemblies; congregations)*," Jesus had warned, "yea, the time comes, that whosoever kills you will think that he does God service. And these things will they do unto you, because they have not known the Father, nor me," John 16:2-3. In this service were the Popes engaged and peoples and princes compelled by either fear or malice.

Even so, those whose hearts were awaken and enlivened by the hearing of the Word of God—Christians indeed—even in the midst of such extremities, persevered in faith and patiently entrusted both their earthly and eternal fates to God. Just as the holy men and women of the Bible, they committed themselves to the Almighty and by their "patient continuance in well doing," (Romans 2:7), joined that "great cloud of witnesses," who, to the refining of their own souls and as a perpetual example to those who would come after them, suffered the rage of this world against God's very Spirit within them. They "were tortured, not accepting deliverance; that they might obtain a better resurrection." They endured, "trial of cruel mockings and scourgings, yea, moreover of bonds and imprisonment: they were stoned, they were sawn asunder, were tempted, were slain with the sword: they wandered about in sheepskins and goatskins; being destitute, afflicted, tormented; (of whom the world was not worthy:) they wandered in deserts, and in mountains, and in dens and caves of the earth," Hebrews 11:35-38.

Like the author of our narrative, many were able to follow the instruction of that great command, "When they persecute you in this city, flee into another," Matthew 10:23. Eventually, by the good hand of God and according to his appointed times and seasons, through the use of lawful means and by that courage which accompanies righteousness, prisoners, peoples, and princes stood against the injustices inflicted upon the Protestants and eventually gained the cessation of even those remote strongholds of injustice as were found in the prisons and Galleys of France. The very freedom of conscience and worship that we enjoy today was only won through such singular moments in history.

We may hope that today, none can any longer be doomed to exile or slavery or death, or commanded by state or statute to profess a creed which they abhor, or to set aside the Scripture to which their heart is captive.

Yet, it will still be the part of every true Christian to be rejected by the world and to suffer persecution, in varying degrees. And like those witnesses who went before us, if we are indeed the children of God, we will both know the truth and understand it, and we will practice it and live by it, and in so doing, we will each suffer for the sake of it. For, "all that will live godly in Christ Jesus shall suffer persecution," 2 Timothy 3:12. Some will be sneered at, others frowned upon, some discountenanced or rejected by friends, some may even be banished from their homes or, in some regions of the world, imprisoned or even slain for their conscientious adherence to a Gospel faith. By these things we are attested to be the children of God for, "The Spirit itself bears witness with our spirit, that we are the children of God: and if children, then heirs; heirs of God, and joint-heirs with Christ; if so be that we suffer with him, that we may be also glorified together," Romans 8:16-17. "It is a faithful saying," says the Apostle Paul, "for if we be dead with him, we shall also live with him: if we suffer, we shall also reign with him," 2 Timothy 2:11-12.

Through all the troubles of this life, we must remember that the sorrows of God's children are for their benefit: "I reckon that the sufferings of this present time are not worthy to be compared with the glory which shall be revealed in us," Romans 8:18-19. The beginning and end of every affliction, and the determined will of God in them, is to effect our eternal good and his eternal glory. "Consider," says Thomas Brooks, "that all your afflictions, troubles, and trials shall work for your good: 'And we know that all things shall work together for good to them that love God,' Romans 8:28. Why then should any fret, fling, and fume, seeing that God designs good for you in all? The bee sucks sweet honey out of the bitterest herbs; so God will by afflictions teach his children to suck sweet knowledge, sweet obedience, and sweet experiences, out of all the bitter afflictions and trials he exercises them with. That scouring and rubbing,[1] which causes others to fret, shall make his children shine the brighter; and that weight which crushes and keeps others under, shall but make his children grow better and higher; and that hammer which knocks others all in pieces, shall but knock his children the nearer to Christ, the corner stone."[2]

"Our faithful and good Shepherd affords to us," says John Newton, "strength according to our day. He knows our frame, and will lay no more on us than he will enable us to bear; yea, I trust, no more than he will cause to work for our good." "Our comforts," he continues, "come free and undeserved. But, when we are afflicted, it is because there is a need for it. He does it not willingly. Our trials are either salutary medicines, or honorable appointments, to put us in such circumstances as may best qualify us to show forth his praise."[3]

We pray that all those who suffer for the sake of the truth call to mind the words of the Apostle: "For it is better, if the will of God be so, that you suffer for well doing, than for evil doing," 1 Peter 3:17. And we pray that those who suffer for the sake of the truth have the kindness and help of their fellow Christians, whose sincere desire and delight is to witness their public and

---

1. Upbraiding and reproaching.

2. Thomas Brooks (1608-1680), *The Mute Christian under the Smarting Rod.*

3. John Newton (1725-1807), *Works,* Letter I.

persevering profession of faith in the atonement and righteousness of the Lord Jesus Christ, together with their grateful obedience to his commands.

Let us end with the consideration of whether we, in a similar trial of our principles, as we see Jean Martielhe and his companions endured for the faith of Jesus Christ in their slavery and torments, would hold as firmly as these youths did then.

Protected, as many of us are, by a kind Providence on every side, we might readily affirm our own readiness with confidence. It becomes us the more to entreat our heavenly Father, "Lead us not into temptation," Luke 11:4. It becomes us to give diligent heed to our Savior's words, "Watch and pray, lest you enter into temptation. The spirit truly is ready, but the flesh is weak," Mark 14:38. And it becomes us constantly to regard the Apostle's exhortation, "Looking unto Jesus the author and finisher of our faith," Hebrews 12:2.

Further, we must observe how much advantage in the hour of trial all those have who heartily love and obey the truth. "Though our outward man perish, yet the inward man is renewed day by day. For our light affliction, which is but for a moment, works for us a far more exceeding and eternal weight of glory," 2 Corinthians 4:17. These are they in whose hearts the grace of God rules and the truths and promises of the Bible are received as the very Words of God; who, in singleness of mind diligently lament and grieve over sin; who "show the work of the law written in their hearts, their conscience also bearing witness, and their thoughts the mean while accusing or else excusing one another," Romans 2:15; who are attached not to an outward principle of Christ, but are compelled by the interior principle of the Spirit and truth of Jesus Christ.

These have within themselves the manifest supports and consolations from above which enabled them to rejoice in tribulations. "For whether we live, we live unto the Lord; and whether we die, we die unto the Lord: whether we live therefore, or die, we are the Lord's," Romans 14:8. These will always be found rejoicing amidst trouble, giving God the glory for strengthening them in weakness, and declaring the glory of God even in the worst injustice, trusting all, their very lives, to that saving faith, "Being justified freely by his grace through the redemption that is in Christ Jesus," Romans 3:24.

The End

FURTHER READING

The Martyrdom of a People; or the Vaudois
of Piedmont and their History
by Henry Fliedner
(2010 Edition by Hail & Fire)

History of the Huguenots
by the American Sunday School Union

The Lollards
by The Religious Tract Society

The Church in the Desert, or Huguenot
Heroes and Martyrs
by W. H. Withrow

The Israel of the Alps; History of the
Vaudois of Piedmont
by Alexis Muston (1857)

The History of the Waldenses
by Jean Paul Perrin (1624)

Condemned to the Galleys: The
Adventures of a French Protestant
by Jean Martielhe (unabridged)

*Find more on our website at
www.hailandfire.com*

Piety is exceeding useful for all sorts of men, in all capacities, all states, all relations; fitting and disposing them to manage all their respective concernments, to discharge all their peculiar duties, in a proper, just, and decent manner. It renders all superiors equal and moderate in their administrations; mild, courteous, and affable in their converse; benign and condescending in all their demeanor toward their inferiors. Correspondingly it disposes inferiors to be sincere and faithful, modest, loving, respectful, diligent, apt willingly to yield due subjection and service. It inclines princes to be just, gentle, benign, careful for their subjects' good, apt to administer justice uprightly, to protect right, to encourage virtue, to check wickedness. Answerably it renders subjects loyal, submissive, obedient, quiet, and peaceable, ready to yield due honor, to pay the tributes and bear the burdens imposed, to discharge all duties, and observe all laws prescribed by their government, conscionably, patiently, cheerfully, without reluctance, grudging, or murmuring.

Rev. Isaac Barrow *(1630-1677)*
The Profitableness of Godliness

"By manifestation of the truth commending ourselves to every
man's conscience in the sight of God."
2 Corinthians 4:2

HAIL & FIRE

Hail & Fire is a resource for Reformed and Gospel
Theology in the works, exhortations, prayers,
and apologetics of those who have
maintained the Gospel and
expounded upon the
Scripture
as the Eternal Word of God
and the sole authority in Christian doctrine.

For the edification of those who hold the Gospel
in truth and for the examination of every
conscience, Hail & Fire reprints
and republishes, in print
and online,
Christian,
Puritan, Reformed
and Protestant sermons and
exhortative works; Protestant and
Catholic polemical and apologetic works;
Bibles, histories, martyrologies, and eschatological works.

Visit us online: www.hailandfire.com

CPSIA information can be obtained
at www.ICGtesting.com
Printed in the USA
LVOW13s0420011216
515261LV00009B/47/P